RACHAEL RAY
30-MINUTE GET REAL MEALS

RACHAEL RAY
30-MINUTE GET REAL MEALS

EAT HEALTHY WITHOUT GOING TO EXTREMES

Clarkson Potter/Publishers
New York

Other Books by Rachael Ray

Rachael Ray's 30-Minute Meals: Cooking 'Round the Clock
Rachael Ray's 30-Minute Meals for Kids: Cooking Rocks!
$40 a Day: Best Eats in Town
Get Togethers: Rachael Ray's 30-Minute Meals
30-Minute Meals 2
Veggie Meals
Comfort Foods
Rachael Ray's Open House Cookbook
30-Minute Meals

Copyright © 2005 by Rachael Ray
Photographs copyright © 2005 by Ben Fink
Food and prop styling by Roscoe Betsill

Published in the United States by Clarkson Potter/
Publishers, New York, an imprint of the Crown Publishing
Group, a division of Random House, Inc.
www.crownpublishing.com
www.clarksonpotter.com

CLARKSON N. POTTER is a trademark and POTTER
and colophon are registered trademarks of Random House,
Inc.

Printed in the United States of America

Design by Jennifer K. Beal

Library of Congress Cataloging-in-Publication Data is
available upon request

ISBN 1-4000-8253-6

10   9   8   7   6   5   4   3   2   1

First Edition

To my Gran'pa Emmanuel. He is no longer with us, but in writing this book, I have come to realize he was a real fore-runner in low-carb cooking. My Gran'pa Emmanuel had diabetes but he never gave up his pasta or bread. He made pastas that were high in protein and full of vegetables with just a little pasta mixed in. He made things sweet with fruit, fresh or dried, or a drizzle of honey, rather than with refined sugar. He grew tons of fruits and vegetables and nuts and kept his recipes down to earth: simple and full of herbs and stocks. Every one of these lower-carb recipes only echoes his thinking, his teachings, and his cooking. How lucky am I to have had such a good example! I think he's been reading these recipes over my shoulder and I hope he's smiling and maybe a little hungry, too!

Thank-You Notes

Thanks to Emily, who helps me embrace all the hard stuff, like low-carb cooking. You rule! I like you as much as spaghetti!

Thanks to Wes for helping me embrace almost-baking. This is the first time 30-minute desserts have appeared in a book of mine. If you like them, send Wes a sweet thank-you note, too.

Thanks as always to the army of talented people who work at turning my piles of computer files full of craziness into pretty books and shiny TV shows.

Thanks to my family for not disowning me during the grumpy days of writing book number ten! I love you all and, Mom, your food remains the best on earth!

Thanks to my yummy fella, John. Just thanks, ya know, for whatever and all of it.

Thanks to my beloved dog, Boo, who always supported her very busy mom. You were the tastiest treat ever!

Contents

Confessions

I confess...

As you are reading this, I'm willing to bet that I have just eaten, and that whatever it was I ate, I had a big bowl of it and it contained carbs. I cannot and will not eat without them.

I confess...

On the other hand, when I do eat fewer carbs, I get to buy and wear better clothes because I look better in them.

I confess...

I do not like extremes, especially when it comes to my food. I have been working in food for twenty years now and I have barely survived the crazy trends: from the teeny-tiny mini portions of Nouvelle "Cuisine" (more like snacks) to the megasize portions of tasteless, sugar-enriched, barklike offerings of the "fat-free" years.

Still, I've always been customer oriented. The public is always right when you grow up in the hospitality business. So, I developed a personal strategy over the years of taking an extreme trend and teaching recipes that reined in the concept yet creatively attempted to respect the principles of the movement. In fact, I originally designed 30-Minute Meals as a cooking class to sell more groceries because the trend of the early 1990s seemed to be no one has any time for anything, period.

Low-carb has been the toughest trend to weather, hands down. I have been miserable and angry for months, trying to churn out pastaless, bread-less, tomato- and fruitless food for the show. One night I just screamed, in a very *Network* moment, "Enough, already!"

So, I came to a very happy place: low-er rather than no-carb 30-Minute Meals. In this book (the biggest challenge for me and my pots to date), you'll find lower-carb living is easy when you can have takeout-style foods, burgers, and yes, even pastas! I have an entire section of pasta dinners that are mostly meats and veggies and just a half pound of pasta per every four adult entrées! Would you rather eat "low-carb" cardboard fake pasta pre-cooked and packaged with eight net carbs or a couple of spoonfuls of the real deal mixed in with veggies and protein? (See, I'm going to win you over here, right? All things, *in moderation*! It's a cliché for a reason.)

Bottom line: Eat fewer carbs and maintain a better bottom, waist, and everything else. But, do not go to such extremes that you deny yourself and those who eat with you to the point of damaging your relationships, your own personality, and possibly your health. Try eating fewer carbs and moving more and I bet you'll feel as good as you look for as long as you like!

RACHAEL RAY
30-MINUTE GET REAL MEALS

CHAPTER 1

SNACKS AND SUPER-SUPPER SNACKS

There are some things tastier than pretzels and chips.

(No, really, there are.) Here are munchies and megamunchy
simple meals that make eating lower carbs a good deal!

Shrimp and Pork Balls with Spicy Lime Dipping Sauce

A lower-carb alternative to pot stickers and other dumplings.

24 BALLS, UP TO 4 SERVINGS OF 6 BALLS EACH

- 4 scallions, green and white parts, coarsely chopped
- 2-inch piece fresh gingerroot, peeled and grated or minced
- 1 serrano or jalapeño chili pepper, seeded and finely chopped, divided
- 2 garlic cloves, crushed
- 1/4 cup plus 3 tablespoons tamari (dark aged soy sauce, found on the international aisle), divided
- 1/4 cup fresh cilantro leaves (a big handful)
- Zest and juice of 2 limes
- 1/2 pound medium shrimp, shelled and deveined, tails removed
- 1 pound ground pork
- 2 to 3 tablespoons vegetable oil
- 1 teaspoon toasted sesame oil
- 1 tablespoon honey
- 2 to 3 tablespoons water
- Toothpicks

In the bowl of a food processor combine the scallions, half of the ginger, half of the chopped chili pepper, the garlic, 3 tablespoons of the tamari, the cilantro, and the lime zest. Pulse for 30 seconds, scrape down the bowl, and then continue to process for 1 minute or until finely ground. Add the shrimp and pork and process until the shrimp are ground into small pieces and the mixture is well combined but not so fine that it becomes a paste, about 1 minute. Roll the shrimp and pork mixture into 24 balls about the size of large walnuts. If you dip your hands in water before rolling the mixture, the rolling goes a little easier.

continued ....➤

Preheat a large nonstick skillet with the vegetable oil over medium heat. Add the balls and don't move them until they are browned on one side, about 2 minutes. Turn the balls and continue to cook, browning on all sides until cooked through, about 3 to 4 minutes longer.

While the balls are cooking, make the spicy lime dipping sauce: In a bowl combine the remaining ginger and chili pepper, the remaining tamari, the lime juice, sesame oil, honey, and 2 tablespoons of water. Taste and adjust the seasoning; if you find it to be too salty, add a little more water and a smidgen more honey.

Arrange the shrimp and pork balls on a platter with a bowl of the spicy lime dipping sauce and a bunch of toothpicks. Spear a ball with a toothpick, dip in the sauce, and eat.

Honey Mustard Chicken Wings

Unreal! Forget Buffalo wings—not only are these healthier than deep-fried wings and way lower in fat, they simply are the best chicken wings you'll ever have! They are super, über-snacks that can be a simple supper, with salad or veggies on the side. The only carbs come from natural juice and honey. Unlike the small, snipped wings served in some bars and restaurants, homemade wings are larger and have more meat. Allow three or four for a full dinner portion per person, though my sweetie and I can eat all twelve if we're watching a double feature that night!

4 SERVINGS, 3 WINGS PER PERSON

- 12 whole chicken wings from meat case of market (drumettes and tips)
  Salt and freshly ground black pepper
- 2 tablespoons vegetable oil (2 turns of the pan)
- ¼ to ⅓ cup spicy deli mustard (eyeball it)
- ½ cup orange juice
  2-inch piece fresh gingerroot, peeled
- 2 tablespoons hot sauce (eyeball it)

2 tablespoons soy sauce (eyeball it)

½ teaspoon crushed hot red pepper flakes

  3 tablespoons honey (a healthy drizzle)

¼ cup chopped fresh cilantro or flat-leaf parsley (a handful)

  2 to 3 tablespoons chopped chives

Preheat the oven to 400°F.

Preheat a large ovenproof skillet over high heat. Liberally season the chicken wings with salt and pepper. Once the skillet is screaming hot add the oil, then the wings in a single, even layer. Brown the wings for 3 minutes per side.

While the wings are browning, assemble the sauce: In a small pot combine the mustard, orange juice, ginger, hot sauce, soy sauce, hot red pepper flakes, and honey. Bring up to a simmer over high heat, then lower the heat, and keep the sauce warm until the wings are done browning. Remove the ginger from the sauce.

After the wings brown, drain off some of the fat and drippings.

Pour the simmering sauce over the browned wings. Place the skillet in the oven and roast the wings for 20 minutes, flipping them once halfway through the cooking time.

Remove the wings from the oven. Toss the wings around in the sauce and finish with the fresh cilantro or parsley and the chives.

Serve hot or at room temperature.

TIDBIT

Close that door! Whenever you are tending to something in the oven, pull it out of the oven completely and close that door while you are doing your business. Otherwise your oven will have to work double time to get back up to temp.

LETTUCE WRAPS

Better than burritos and tacos, these wraps have crunch and the lettuce lets the flavors of the fillings shine through.

MYOTO: MAKE YOUR OWN TAKEOUT

Chinese Chicken Lettuce Wraps

4 SERVINGS

2 cups (4 handfuls) fresh shiitake mushrooms

1⅓ to 1½ pounds thin-cut chicken breast or chicken tenders

2 tablespoons light-colored oil, such as vegetable or peanut oil (2 turns of the pan)

Coarse salt and coarse black pepper

3 garlic cloves, chopped

1-inch piece gingerroot, peeled and finely chopped or grated (optional)

1 orange (you'll use the zest)

½ red bell pepper, diced small

1 can (8 ounces) sliced water chestnuts, drained and chopped

3 scallions, chopped

3 tablespoons hoisin sauce (Chinese barbecue sauce, available on Asian foods aisle of market)

½ head iceberg lettuce, core removed, quartered

1 head of Boston or Bibb lettuce, leaves separated

Wedges of navel orange, for garnish

Remove the tough stems from the mushrooms and brush with a damp towel to clean; slice the mushrooms. Chop the chicken into small pieces.

Preheat a large skillet or wok to high.

Add the oil to the hot pan. Add the chicken to the pan and sear the meat by stir-frying for a minute or two. Add the mushrooms and cook for another minute or two. Season with salt and pepper, then add the garlic and ginger. Cook for a minute more. Grate the orange zest into the pan, add the bell pepper bits, water chestnuts, and scallions. Cook for another minute, continuing to stir-fry the mixture. Add the hoisin sauce and toss to coat the mixture evenly. Transfer the hot chopped barbecued chicken to a serving platter and pile the quartered wedges of crisp iceberg lettuce alongside. Add the wedged oranges to the platter to garnish. To eat, pile spoonfuls into the lettuce leaves and squeeze an orange wedge over. Fold up the wrap and eat.

Paco's Fish Tacos in Lettuce Wraps

4 SERVINGS

Cooking spray
2 pounds halibut or grouper fillets
Salt and freshly ground black pepper
Bibb or green leaf lettuce leaves, for wrapping
1 jalapeño, seeded and chopped
1 cup cilantro leaves (stems removed)
3 sprigs fresh mint
3 tablespoons grainy mustard
2 tablespoons red wine vinegar
¼ cup extra-virgin olive oil (EVOO) (eyeball it)
1 lime
Hot sauce, such as Tabasco
½ red onion, finely chopped

Heat a grill pan or nonstick skillet over high heat. Spray the pan with cooking spray. Place the fish on the grill pan, season with

continued ....➤

salt and pepper, and cook for 5 minutes on each side, or until opaque. Transfer to a serving plate.

Arrange the lettuce leaves on a platter. Place the jalapeño in a food processor with the cilantro, mint, mustard, and vinegar. Turn on the processor and stream in the EVOO, then season the sauce with salt and pepper.

Break the fish into chunks and squeeze lime juice over the fish. Add a few dashes of hot sauce.

Pile the fish in lettuce leaves and top each "taco" with the jalapeño cilantro sauce and chopped red onions.

Guacamole Salad

4 SERVINGS

- 2 medium Hass avocados, pitted and sliced
- 2 medium tomatoes, seeded and chopped
- $\frac{1}{2}$ English (seedless) cucumber (the one wrapped in plastic), chopped
- $\frac{1}{2}$ red onion, sliced
- 1 jalapeño, seeded and finely chopped
- 3 tablespoons fresh lemon juice
- 1 small garlic clove, chopped
  A few drops of hot sauce, such as Tabasco
- 1 teaspoon salt
- $\frac{1}{3}$ cup extra-virgin olive oil (EVOO) (eyeball it)

Arrange the vegetables on a platter. Whisk the lemon juice with the garlic, a few drops of hot sauce, and the salt, then stream the EVOO into the dressing while whisking. Pour the lemon dressing over the salad and serve.

Shrimp and Scallops with Bacon

4 SERVINGS

- 12 raw jumbo shrimp, peeled and deveined (16 to 20 count per pound)
- 12 raw large sea scallops, trimmed and well drained
-     Zest and juice of 1 lime
- 1 tablespoon toasted sesame oil (a generous drizzle)
- 1 tablespoon grill seasoning, such as McCormick's Montreal Steak Seasoning, or coarse salt and freshly ground black pepper
- 1 teaspoon hot red pepper flakes
- 12 slices center-cut or applewood-smoked bacon, cut in half
-     Toothpicks
- 3 scallions, very thinly sliced on an angle

Preheat the oven to 425°F.

Place the shrimp and scallops in a shallow dish or bowl. Dress the seafood with the lime juice and zest, sesame oil, grill seasoning, and hot red pepper flakes. Wrap each shrimp and scallop with a half slice of bacon. Wrap each shrimp from head to tail, pulling the bacon snuggly around the shrimp. Wrap the bacon around the outside of each scallop. Fasten the bacon in place with toothpicks.

Arrange the shrimp and scallops on a slotted baking pan, such as a broiler pan, to allow it to drain while the bacon crisps. Bake for 10 to 14 minutes, until the shrimp is pink and curled, the scallops are opaque, and the bacon is crisp. Check after 8 minutes; the shrimp might finish before the scallops.

Arrange the cooked seafood on a platter and sprinkle with chopped scallions.

Caesar Salad to Go: Shrimp or Chicken Lettuce Wraps with Creamy Caesar Dressing

This recipe requires no cooking and is served cold, so it makes a perfect low-carb on-the-go lunch, or a picnic for the park as well! Pack the dressing with an ice pack to keep it chilled out.

If you think you don't like anchovies, try them in this dressing. They just taste salty and yummy!

4 SERVINGS

- 2 romaine lettuce hearts
- 1 pound fully cooked jumbo shrimp (from the seafood counter)
- 1 rotisserie chicken (available in many markets)
- 4 heaping tablespoons reduced-fat mayonnaise
- 1 garlic clove, crushed
  Zest and juice of 1 lemon
- 2 tablespoons anchovy paste (optional—but the salad tastes better with it in)
- ½ cup grated Parmigiano-Reggiano or Parmesan (a few handfuls)
- 2 teaspoons Worcestershire sauce (eyeball the amount)
- 1 teaspoon coarse black pepper (eyeball it)
- 3 tablespoons extra-virgin olive oil (EVOO) (pour to the count of 4)

Cut the bottoms off the romaine and cut the hearts in half lengthwise. Wash the lettuce and separate the leaves. Let it dry in the dish draining rack while you prepare the rest of the menu.

Remove the tails from the shrimp and place the shrimp in a bowl or, if this is a picnic meal, pack for travel.

To remove the chicken meat from the chicken, cut the chicken breasts off first. Cut the legs and thighs off using kitchen scissors.

Slice the meat up on an angle. Arrange on a plate or in a plastic container.

Place the mayo, garlic, lemon zest and juice, anchovy paste, cheese, Worcestershire, and pepper in the blender and turn it on. Stream the EVOO into the dressing through the center of the lid. When the dressing is combined, use a rubber spatula to remove the thick dressing to a bowl or a plastic container.

Place the lettuce on a serving platter or pack in a large plastic bag or container to travel.

To assemble, spread some dressing onto a lettuce leaf. Fill the leaf with a large shrimp or sliced cold chicken, like a lettuce taco, and eat!

Grilled Shrimp and Rémoulade Sauce

SERVES UP TO 4 FOR SNACKS

3	tablespoons extra-virgin olive oil (EVOO)
	Zest and juice of 1 orange
	Salt and freshly ground black pepper
16	raw large shrimp, peeled, leaving the tail on, and deveined
1½	cups mayonnaise
4	tablespoons Creole mustard or grainy mustard
¼	yellow onion, grated
2	celery ribs, very finely minced
1	rounded tablespoon prepared horseradish
1	tablespoon Worcestershire sauce
1	teaspoon hot sauce, such as Tabasco
1	teaspoon paprika (⅓ palmful)
	A handful fresh flat-leaf parsley, chopped

continued ....➤

Preheat an outdoor grill or stovetop grill pan to high heat.

In a bowl, combine the EVOO, orange juice and zest, and salt and pepper to taste. Add the shrimp and toss to coat the shrimp completely. Place the shrimp on the grill and cook for 3 minutes each side, or until the shrimp are pink and have curled up. Remove the shrimp from the grill onto a baking sheet or large plate in a single layer. Place in the refrigerator to chill.

In a bowl, combine the mayonnaise, Creole mustard, grated onion, celery, horseradish, Worcestershire sauce, hot sauce, paprika, and parsley. Store the rémoulade sauce in the refrigerator until the shrimp are chilled.

To serve, surround a bowl of the rémoulade sauce with the chilled grilled shrimp.

TIDBITS

If you are not into grilling, you can prepare the shrimp in a large nonstick skillet.

For a surf-and-turf version, wrap the chilled piece of cooked shrimp in a half slice of thin roast beef from the deli counter.

Get in the habit of measuring by eye. One teaspoon of coarse black pepper is equal to about a third of a palmful.

New England Shrimp and Lobster Lettuce Rolls

4 SERVINGS

- 16 raw jumbo shrimp, peeled and deveined
- 1 medium zucchini, sliced lengthwise into long, $1/2$-inch-thick slices
  Extra-virgin olive oil (EVOO), for drizzling
  Salt and freshly ground black pepper
- 1 celery rib, finely chopped
  Juice of 1 lemon
- $1/2$ to $3/4$ cup mayonnaise (eyeball it)
- $1/2$ small yellow onion, grated
  Several dashes of hot sauce, such as Tabasco
- 1 large half-sour or dill pickle, finely chopped
- 2 tablespoons capers, drained and roughly chopped
- 3 sprigs fresh tarragon, leaves stripped and chopped, about 2 tablespoons
- 1 handful fresh flat-leaf parsley, chopped
- 2 small cooked lobster tails, about 10 to 12 ounces total, or 1 tub (8 ounces) cooked lobster meat (available at some fish counters)
- 12 grape tomatoes, halved
- 1 head Boston or Bibb lettuce, leaves separated

Preheat an outdoor grill or indoor grill pan over high heat.

Place the shrimp in one bowl, the zucchini in another. Drizzle both the shrimp and zucchini with a little EVOO, then season with salt and pepper. Toss to coat completely. Grill the shrimp for 2 minutes on each side, until opaque. Grill the zucchini slices for 2 minutes on each side or until darkly marked by the grill. Remove both the shrimp and zucchini from the grill to cool.

While the shrimp and zucchini are cooling, make the tartar sauce. In a medium bowl combine the celery, lemon juice, mayonnaise, grated onion, hot sauce, pickle, capers, tarragon, parsley, and salt and pepper.

continued ....➤

Chop the cooled shrimp and zucchini into bite-size pieces. Chop the lobster meat the same way. Add the chopped shrimp, zucchini, lobster, and grape tomatoes to the tartar sauce and mix to combine. Arrange the lettuce leaves on a platter and fill each leaf with the shrimp and lobster mixture. Roll up and enjoy.

Zippy Ham Salad Cucumber Snackers

4 SERVINGS

¼ pound cooked deli ham, sliced ¼ inch thick, finely diced
1 celery rib, from the heart, finely chopped
A couple of spoonfuls of green salad olives with pimiento, drained, finely chopped
2 tablespoons chopped fresh flat-leaf parsley
2 tablespoons mayonnaise (just enough to bind the salad)
1 tablespoon prepared yellow mustard
1 large dill pickle, finely chopped
¼ small red onion, finely chopped
Salt and freshly ground black pepper
1 long English (seedless) cucumber (the one wrapped in plastic)

In a bowl combine the ham, celery, olives, parsley, mayonnaise, mustard, pickle, red onion, and salt and pepper to taste. Reserve.

Cut the cucumber into 1½-inch-thick disks. With a melon baller scoop out a little bit of the center of each cucumber disk to create a cup. Fill each cup with a heaping tablespoon of the ham salad. Serve cold.

Everything Roasted Nuts

As satisfying to me as a big, chewy, still-hot everything bagel schmeared with lots of cream cheese, but these have better crunch and way less carbs!

3 CUPS

- 1 cup blanched (skinned) whole almonds (available in bulk foods section of market)
- 1 cup whole hazelnuts (available in bulk foods section of market)
- 2 tablespoons butter
- 1 tablespoon grill seasoning (a palmful; such as McCormick's Montreal Steak Seasoning)
- 1 teaspoon granulated garlic or garlic powder ($1/3$ palmful)
- $1^{1}/_{2}$ teaspoons ground cumin (half a palmful)
- 1 tablespoon hot sauce (eyeball it)
- 1 cup smoked almonds, such as Diamond brand (available on the snack aisle)
- 1 teaspoon poppy seeds ($1/3$ palmful)
- 1 tablespoon sesame seeds (a palmful)

Preheat the oven or toaster oven to 400°F. Roast the peeled almonds and hazelnuts for about 7 to 8 minutes; your nose will know when they're done.

Melt the butter in a large skillet over low heat and add the seasoning mix, garlic, cumin, and hot sauce. Add the roasted nuts and smoked almonds to the pan and toss to coat in the butter. Add the poppy seeds and sesame seeds, sprinkling them over the nuts; transfer to a small bowl and serve warm.

Ham and Herb Cheese Cucumber Snackers

4 SERVINGS, 4 PIECES EACH

- 1/2 English (seedless) cucumber (the one wrapped in plastic)
  Salt and freshly ground black pepper
- 1 6-ounce package Boursin cheese with garlic and herbs (available in the dairy case at many supermarkets)
- 3 or 4 slices French ham or deli-sliced boiled ham

Cut 16 1/2-inch-thick pieces of cucumber on a bit of an angle and add salt and pepper to taste. Spread some Boursin cheese on the cucumber slices. Cut the ham into 2-inch strips. Wrap a strip of ham around each cucumber slice, covering the cheese.

Raw Tuna Snackers on Daikon

16 PIECES

- 1 pound sushi-grade ahi tuna
- 1/4 cup tamari (dark aged soy sauce, found on the international aisle)
- 1 teaspoon wasabi paste (international aisle again)
- 3 tablespoons sesame seeds
- 2 daikon (5 to 6 ounces each), thinly sliced into 16 pieces, or 4 large red radishes, sliced
- 2 scallions, very thinly sliced on an angle

Slice the tuna into 16 1/4-inch-thick rectangular pieces. Mix the tamari and wasabi together and combine thoroughly. Pass the tuna slices through the soy mixture and dot the tuna slices on both sides with a pile of sesame seeds. Place each piece of tuna onto a slice of daikon or red radish and top with a few pieces of sliced scallion.

Warm Cheese with Endive and Cauliflower

4 SERVINGS

1 1-pound wheel Brie cheese or ¼ kilo wheel of Camembert cheese
1 small endive, leaves separated
1½ to 2 cups cauliflower florets (½ head)

Cut the top rind off the Brie or Camembert and place it on a plate. Heat the cheese in the microwave on High until the cheese is hot and becoming liquidlike. Depending on the ripeness of the cheese, it will take anywhere from 60 to 90 seconds on High to melt it.

Serve the warm, softened cheese with the endive leaves and cauliflower for dunking and spooning up the double-cream deliciousness! If the cheese tightens up, reheat it for 20 to 30 seconds on High.

Ham and Cheese Mini Frittatas

Baby Lamb Chops with Artichoke and Tarragon Dip

Crab Salad Bites on Endive

Ham and Cheese Mini Frittatas

Quiche—hold the crust and the work!

12 MINI FRITTATAS

- 3 tablespoons melted butter
- ¼ pound deli-sliced Swiss cheese, finely chopped
- ¼ pound ham steak or Canadian bacon, finely chopped
- A splash of milk or half-and-half
- 3 tablespoons snipped or chopped fresh chives
- Salt and freshly ground black pepper
- A few drops of hot sauce
- 8 large eggs, well beaten

Preheat the oven to 375°F.

Brush a 12-muffin tin liberally with the butter. Divide the chopped cheese and ham evenly among the muffin cups. Add the milk, chives, salt and pepper, and hot sauce to the eggs and fill the cups up to just below the rim with the egg mixture. Bake the frittatas until golden and puffy, 10 to 12 minutes. Remove to a plate with a small spatula and serve.

Alternative fillings: You can also try defrosted chopped frozen broccoli and shredded Cheddar, or chopped cooked bacon with shredded smoked Gouda and sautéed mushrooms.

Baby Lamb Chops with Artichoke and Tarragon Dip

24 CHOPS, 6 TO 8 SERVINGS

- 1 can (15 ounces) quartered artichoke hearts in water, drained
- 1 jar (6 ounces) marinated baby mushrooms and their liquid
- 1 shallot, coarsely chopped
- 4 sprigs fresh tarragon, stripped, plus a few sprigs for garnish
- 3 tablespoons white wine vinegar
  Salt and freshly ground black pepper
- 1/2 cup extra-virgin olive oil (EVOO), plus some for drizzling
- 24 baby lamb chops (get the butcher to cut them)
- 1/2 pound baby cut carrots (available in produce department)
- 1/2 pound sugar snap peas
- 4 radishes, cleaned and trimmed but left on greens, halved lengthwise

Preheat a broiler or grill pan to high.

In a food processor, combine the artichokes, marinated mushrooms, shallot, tarragon, and vinegar. Season with salt and pepper and turn the processor on; stream in about 1/2 cup of the EVOO until a spoonable, fairly smooth dip forms, about 1 minute. Scrape the dip into a serving bowl and place a demitasse (small) spoon in the dip so it can be easily dolloped onto each individual lamb chop when they're served.

Drizzle the chops with a few teaspoons of EVOO and season with salt and pepper. Grill or broil for 2 minutes on each side and remove to rest.

To serve, place the dip on a large platter or cutting board and surround with the cooked chops and piles of baby cut carrots, sugar snap peas, and halved radishes for dipping and topping. Garnish the platter with additional sprigs of tarragon.

Crab Salad Bites on Endive

24 PIECES, 6 TO 8 SERVINGS

- 6 ounces lump white crabmeat
- ¼ red bell pepper, finely chopped
- 1 shallot, finely chopped
  Zest of 1 orange
- 3 radishes, grated
- 3 tablespoons chopped celery leaves
  Salt and freshly ground black pepper
- ¼ cup mayonnaise
- 3 tablespoons heavy cream
- 24 leaves Belgian endive
  Chopped fresh flat-leaf parsley or chives, for garnish

Place the crab in a medium bowl and use your fingertips to break it into small pieces. Add the bell pepper, shallot, orange zest, grated radish, celery greens, and salt and pepper. Combine the mayonnaise and heavy cream in a small bowl. Add the dressing to the crab and mix well. Mound a rounded spoonful of the crab salad onto the root end of each endive and fill the leaves to half their length. Arrange the stuffed endive on a platter and garnish with chopped parsley or chives.

Draggers

I use this recipe (more like a method, really) as a standard party offering, and it's one of my all-time favorite snackers. I eat mine with flatbread, but it's good to spread these combinations on sliced seedless cucumbers, too.

I SNACK THROUGH A WHOLE BOURSIN IN AN EVENING, EASY. FOR A PARTY, EACH CHEESE WILL SERVE 4 TO 6 PEOPLE, WITH OTHER OFFERINGS.

BASE

1 6-inch round Boursin cheese with garlic and herbs (available in the dairy case at most supermarkets)

TOPPERS

¼ cup prepared basil pesto

3 tablespoons olive tapenade

3 tablespoons sun-dried tomato tapenade

GARNISHES

Chopped fresh basil or flat-leaf parsley

Crushed hot red pepper flakes

CRUNCHY DRAGGERS

Sliced English (seedless) cucumber (the one wrapped in plastic)

Sliced bell pepper

Celery sticks

Sesame flatbreads

Place the Boursin on a large plate. Spread a thick layer of your choice of basil pesto, olive tapenade, or sun-dried tomato tapenade all over the top of the cheese. Garnish is entirely optional, but for parties, you might want to throw a little chopped basil or parsley on the pesto or parsley and hot red pepper flakes on the tapenades.

Surround the cheese with any or all of the draggers. When you drag a piece of vegetable or a flatbread through the cheese, the sauce will slide away and combine with the cheese. YUMMO!

Hummus Dippers

This recipe is great for parties as well as snack attacks. Store-bought hummus has 4 grams of carbs per serving, but sometimes the flavor needs a boost. When I buy a tub of roasted red pepper hummus it has like 10 little pieces of pepper in it. So, I take plain hummus and grind it up with a whole jar of roasted peppers and then I have a red, delicious bowl of a terrific dipper!

1½ TO 2 CUPS

BASE

1 tub (8 ounces) plain, 40-spice, or garlic hummus (try Tribe of Two Sheiks brand)
1 small garlic clove
Juice of ½ lemon

ADD-INS—CHOOSE ONE

1 jar (14 to 16 ounces) roasted red peppers, well drained
8 ounces pitted good-quality green olives
1 can (15 ounces) artichoke hearts in water, well drained

GARNISHES

Chopped fresh flat-leaf parsley or dill
Crushed hot red pepper flakes
Lemon zest

DIPPERS

Sliced English (seedless) cucumber (the one wrapped in plastic)
Cauliflower florets
Broccoli florets
Celery sticks

Combine the hummus in a food processor with the garlic, a little fresh lemon juice, and your choice of roasted red peppers, olives, or artichoke hearts. Process until smooth and transfer to a serving dish. Garnish with your choice of any or all: parsley, dill, crushed red pepper flakes, and lemon zest. Serve with your choice of sliced cucumbers, cauliflower or broccoli florets, and celery sticks.

Mushroom and Red Pepper–Black Olive Tapenade Bites

24 STUFFED MUSHROOMS

- 24 button mushrooms, stems removed
- Salt and freshly ground black pepper
- Extra-virgin olive oil (EVOO), for drizzling
- 1 jar (8 to 9 ounces) roasted red peppers, drained
- ¼ cup fresh flat-leaf parsley leaves (a couple of handfuls)
- ¼ cup kalamata olives, pitted (about 20 olives)
- 2 tablespoons capers, drained
- 1 large garlic clove, cracked
- Zest and juice of 1 lemon (zest it first)
- ½ cup mascarpone cheese, for garnish

Preheat the oven to 350°F.

Toss the mushroom caps in a bowl with some salt, pepper, and a drizzle of EVOO. Arrange the mushrooms on a baking sheet in an even layer with the gill side up. Roast the mushrooms for 10 to 12 minutes, or until they are cooked through.

While the mushrooms are roasting, prepare the red pepper–black olive tapenade. Place the roasted red peppers in a food processor with the parsley. Add the olives, capers, garlic, and lemon zest. Pulse the processor and grind into a paste.

Once the mushrooms are done roasting, squeeze the juice of the lemon over them. Place about ½ tablespoon tapenade in each cap. Use 2 spoons for this: One is to scoop tapenade and the other is to push it off onto the mushroom. Place the mascarpone in a sealable plastic bag. Squeeze the cheese into one of the bottom corners, and with scissors snip ¼ inch off of that corner. Squeeze a little mascarpone on top of each tapenade-filled mushroom. Serve hot or at room temperature.

PORTOBELLO PIZZAS

Mini pizzas, hold the bread, built on roasted portobellos instead!

Vegetable Portobello Pizzas

1 SERVING, 2 MINI PIZZAS

- 2 large portobello mushroom caps, stems removed
  Extra-virgin olive oil (EVOO), for drizzling
- 4 pieces jarred grilled eggplant or marinated eggplant (available on Italian food aisle), drained
- 1 jarred roasted red pepper, drained and sliced
- 4 water-packed artichoke hearts, drained and sliced
- 3 tablespoons chopped fresh flat-leaf parsley or basil
- ½ cup arugula or baby spinach
- ¼ cup finely chopped onion or shallot
  Salt and freshly ground black pepper
- 4 slices deli provolone cheese, or ¼ pound Italian Fontina cheese, sliced
  Crushed hot red pepper flakes
  Italian dried seasoning or dried oregano

Preheat the oven or toaster oven to 450°F. Place the mushroom caps gill side up on a baking sheet and drizzle with EVOO. Roast for 12 minutes, or until tender. Layer the caps with the grilled eggplant, sliced roasted red pepper, sliced artichokes, parsley or basil, and arugula or spinach. Drizzle the tops with a little more EVOO, and sprinkle with finely chopped onion or shallot and salt and pepper. Top the mushrooms with 2 slices provolone or fontina each in even layers, then return the pizzas to the oven. Bake for 5 minutes to set the vegetables and melt the cheese. Add a pinch of red pepper flakes and Italian dried seasoning or oregano to the top of each portobello mini pizza and transfer to a plate.

Sausage Portobello Pizzas

1 SERVING, 2 MINI PIZZAS

- 2 large portobello mushroom caps, stems removed
  Extra-virgin olive oil (EVOO), for drizzling
- 2 links Italian sausage, sweet or hot, split and sausage removed from casing
- ½ cup marinara sauce or pizza sauce
- 4 slices mozzarella or smoked mozzarella cheese
  Crushed hot red pepper flakes
  Italian dried seasoning blend or dried oregano

Preheat the oven or toaster oven to 450°F. Place the mushroom caps gill side up on a baking sheet and drizzle with EVOO. Roast for 12 minutes, or until tender.

Heat a small nonstick skillet over medium to medium-high heat. Add a drizzle of EVOO to the pan and add the sausage. Break up and brown the sausage for 5 to 7 minutes, until no pink remains. Transfer the cooked meat to a plate lined with paper towels to drain.

Remove the caps from the oven or toaster oven and top each of them with a layer of marinara or pizza sauce, cooked sausage, and cheese. Return the caps to the oven and bake for 3 or 4 minutes to melt the cheese and brown it at the edges. Remove the pizzas from the oven and top with a pinch of crushed red pepper flakes and Italian seasoning or dried oregano.

Pepperoni Portobello Pizzas

1 SERVING, 2 MINI PIZZAS

- 2 large portobello mushroom caps, stems removed
  Extra-virgin olive oil (EVOO), for drizzling
  Salt and freshly ground black pepper
- ¼ cup pizza sauce or marinara sauce
- 6 slices sandwich pepperoni (from the deli counter)
- 4 slices mozzarella cheese or smoked mozzarella cheese
  Crushed hot red pepper flakes
  Dried Italian seasoning or dried oregano

Preheat the oven or toaster oven to 450°F. Place the mushroom caps gill side up on a baking sheet and drizzle with EVOO. Roast for 12 minutes, or until tender. Remove the caps from the oven, season with salt and pepper, and top each with a few spoonfuls of pizza sauce or marinara spread out in a thin layer. Top the layer of sauce with layers of pepperoni and mozzarella cheese and return to the hot oven. Cook the pizzas for another 3 or 4 minutes, until the cheese is bubbly and brown at edges. Garnish the pizzas with red pepper flakes and a pinch or two of Italian seasoning blend or dried oregano.

EGG-CELLENT IDEAS

Use all of the following egg recipes at all hours; they make a great late-night/all-night snack, an awesome and unusual breakfast, or a simple dinner when you are totally eggs-hausted!

Egg Roll-ups

1 SERVING

½ tablespoon extra-virgin olive oil (EVOO) (half a turn of the pan)
   Salt and freshly ground black pepper
1 egg, vigorously beaten
3 tablespoons shredded sharp Cheddar or Monterey Jack cheese
1 tablespoon store-bought tomatillo salsa

Preheat an 8- to 9-inch nonstick skillet over medium-low heat with the EVOO. Add a little salt and pepper to the beaten egg, and whisk to combine. Add the seasoned egg to the hot pan. Give the pan a shake to help spread the egg out to cover the bottom of the skillet. Resist the temptation to stir the egg. Cover the pan with a piece of foil and cook for 1 minute. Remove the foil, sprinkle with the grated cheese, return the foil, and continue to cook for 1 to 2 more minutes, or until the egg has completely set and the cheese has melted. Give the pan a good shake to loosen the cooked egg, then bring the pan over to your cutting board. Tilt the pan and shake the egg out onto the cutting board, keeping the egg relatively flat as you shake it from the skillet. Spread the tomatillo salsa across the egg. Roll the egg as tightly as possible, being careful not to tear it. Allow the rolled-up egg to cool slightly, just a minute or so. With a sharp knife cut into 1- to 1½-inch-wide disks. Eat and enjoy.

Other fillings suggestions: smoked salmon and chopped fresh dill; chopped cooked chorizo and Cheddar; sliced deli roast turkey, Swiss cheese, and mustard.

Mini frittatas make a high-protein snack that is like a bread-free Hot Pocket. Be sure to use a small—no more than 6-inch diameter—nonstick skillet to make these.

Ham and Cheese Frittaco

1 SERVING

- 2 to 3 tablespoons extra-virgin olive oil (EVOO) (eyeball it)
- 2 large eggs, beaten
  A splash of half-and-half or milk (1 to 2 tablespoons)
  Salt and freshly ground black pepper
  A few drops of hot sauce, such as Tabasco
- 1 slice, your choice: Swiss, provolone, or slicing Cheddar
- 2 slices deli ham, your choice: baked, smoked, boiled, or prosciutto

Heat a small nonstick skillet with the EVOO over medium-low to medium heat. Beat the eggs with a splash of half-and-half, salt and pepper, and hot sauce. Cook the eggs in the skillet for 2 minutes without disturbing them. Once the eggs have browned and set, flip the frittata. Add a layer of cheese, then the ham, folding it to fit in the pan and cover the surface of the eggs and cheese evenly. Fold the frittata so it looks like a taco, and slide it onto a plate. Eat!

Mexican Frittaco

1 SERVING

- 2 large eggs, beaten
- 1 teaspoon chili powder
   Salt and freshly ground black pepper
   A few drops of hot sauce, such as Tabasco
- 2 to 3 tablespoons extra-virgin olive oil (EVOO) (eyeball it)
- 1 cup (4 ounces) shredded Pepper Jack or chipotle Cheddar cheese, such as Cabot brand
- ½ cup store-bought tomatillo salsa, green chili salsa verde, or smoky chipotle salsa
- ½ avocado, sliced
- 2 teaspoons fresh lemon juice

Beat the eggs together with the chili powder, salt and pepper, and hot sauce. Heat a small nonstick skillet and the EVOO over medium to medium-low heat. Add the eggs and fry without stirring until brown and set, about 2 minutes. Flip the frittata. Top the frittata with cheese and salsa. Sprinkle the sliced avocado with a little lemon juice and arrange the slices across half of the frittata. Fold it over, so it resembles a taco. Slide the completed frittaco on to a plate and eat!

Spanish Frittaco

1 SERVING

- 2 to 3 tablespoons extra-virgin olive oil (EVOO) (eyeball it)
- 2 large eggs, beaten
- 1 shallot, finely chopped
- 2 tablespoons chopped fresh flat-leaf parsley
  Salt and freshly ground black pepper
- 1 teaspoon (several drops) hot sauce, such as Tabasco
- 2 to 3 ounces manchego cheese, thinly sliced (just enough to cover your small frittata)
- 2 slices Serrano ham or prosciutto
- 1 piece roasted red pepper, drained and sliced

Heat a small nonstick skillet over medium heat with the EVOO. Beat the eggs with the shallot, parsley, salt and pepper, and hot sauce, then add to the skillet. Fry the eggs without disturbing them for 2 minutes, or until brown and set. Flip the frittata (invert pan with a plate to help you if necessary). Top the frittata with the cheese, ham, and roasted pepper. Fold the frittata over, like a taco. Slide the frittaco out onto a plate and eat hot or at room temperature.

SCRAMBLES

These are too easy. Scrambles are my favorite go-to snack. You are only limited by your own imagination when it comes to add-ins for scrambled eggs. Here are a few of my favorite combos.

Sunday Morning Salmon Hold-the-Bagel Scrambles

1 SERVING

- 1 tablespoon butter
- 2 large eggs, beaten
- 2 ounces (2 big spoonfuls) cream cheese, softened
- 2 tablespoons chopped fresh chives (optional)
  Salt and freshly ground black pepper
  A couple slices of smoked salmon, cut into strips

Heat a small nonstick skillet over medium-low to medium heat. Melt the butter in the hot skillet and beat the eggs with the cream cheese, chives, salt and pepper, using a whisk. The cream cheese breaks up into little pieces and it makes the eggs look lumpy and kinda gross, but it tastes awesome. Add the eggs to the pan and scramble them up. The cream cheese melts into the eggs and makes them ROCK! Scramble the eggs to desired doneness. Stir in the salmon and transfer to a plate.

Sausage and Provolone Scrambles

For Cheryl.

- 1 tablespoon extra-virgin olive oil (EVOO) (1 turn of the pan)
- 1 patty of Italian sweet sausage or 1 link, split open and casing removed
- 2 eggs, beaten
- 1 teaspoon (several drops) hot sauce, such as Tabasco
  Salt and freshly ground black pepper
- 2 deli slices sharp provolone, cut into 1-inch dice

Heat a small nonstick skillet over medium heat. Add the EVOO and break up the sausage into the pan. Cook until browned all over, about 5 minutes. Beat the eggs with the hot sauce and salt and pepper. Add the eggs to the sausage and scramble to desired doneness. Add the cheese. Loosely cover the skillet with foil and let stand for 30 seconds or so to start the cheese melting over your scrambles. Slide the sausage scrambles onto your plate and eat.

Garlic and Broccoli Scrambles

I always keep a box or bag of chopped broccoli and chopped spinach on hand in the freezer, because they are so useful in so many recipes. If you have trouble separating the broccoli, zap it in the mic on Defrost a couple of minutes.

1 SERVING

2   tablespoons extra-virgin olive oil (EVOO) (eyeball it)
1   large garlic clove, finely chopped
½   teaspoon crushed hot red pepper flakes
1   cup frozen chopped broccoli (a couple handfuls)
    Salt
2   large eggs, beaten
    Freshly ground black pepper
    Shaved Asiago or Parmigiano-Reggiano, for garnish

Heat a small nonstick skillet over medium heat. Add the EVOO, garlic, and red pepper flakes, cook a minute or so, then add the frozen chopped broccoli. When you add the broccoli to the skillet, break it up and let the broc cook off all of its water and fry up a bit at the edges, 3 or 4 minutes. Season the broccoli with a little salt and beat up the eggs with some salt and pepper, too. Add the eggs to the skillet and scramble to desired doneness with the broccoli. Use a vegetable peeler to shave cheese on top of the eggs. YUMMO!

CHAPTER 2
BURGERS GONE WILD!

Stripped of their boring, everyday buns, these burgers are free to make tasty new partnerships.

Now they've become so wildly delicious, those buns can just dry up—they will not be missed!

Lamb Mini Burgers on Mixed Salad with Fennel

4 SERVINGS, 3 MINI BURGERS EACH

1½ pounds ground lamb

2 to 3 tablespoons chopped fresh rosemary

1 large navel orange, zested, then peeled and sectioned or sliced into disks

¼ red onion, finely chopped

Salt and freshly ground black pepper

1 romaine lettuce heart, chopped

1 head radicchio, chopped

¼ red onion, sliced

1 bulb fennel, trimmed of fronds and tops and quartered lengthwise

¼ cup chopped fresh flat-leaf parsley

2 tablespoons red wine vinegar

¼ cup extra-virgin olive oil (EVOO) (eyeball it)

Preheat a grill pan over medium-high heat or preheat the broiler to high. Combine the lamb, rosemary, orange zest, chopped red onion, salt, and pepper. Make 12 balls and flatten them into 3-inch meat patties. Grill for 2 to 3 minutes on each side. Hold the cooked patties on a plate under foil.

Combine the lettuces in a shallow bowl with the sliced onion. Cut the core out of the fennel pieces and thinly slice, then add to the salad. Scatter the oranges and parsley around the salad and dress with the vinegar, oil, salt, and pepper, to your taste. Top portions of the salad with 3 mini lamb patties and serve.

Mini Meatball Burgers on Antipasto Salad

4 SERVINGS, 3 MINI BURGERS EACH

- 1½ pounds ground sirloin or ground beef, pork, and veal, combined
  Salt and freshly ground black pepper
- 1 egg yolk, beaten
- ½ cup grated Parmigiano-Reggiano (a couple handfuls)
- 2 tablespoons tomato paste
  A handful of chopped fresh flat-leaf parsley
- 2 garlic cloves, finely chopped
- ½ to 1 teaspoon crushed hot red pepper flakes
  Extra-virgin olive oil (EVOO) for drizzling, plus about ¼ cup for dressing salad
- 2 romaine lettuce hearts, chopped
- 1 can (15 ounces) quartered artichoke hearts, drained
- 1 jarred roasted red pepper, drained and chopped
- 4 or 5 peperoncini peppers, chopped, or ¼ cup hot banana pepper rings, drained
- ½ cup pitted good-quality olives, green or black, drained
- 3 celery ribs, chopped
- ¼ pound Genoa salami or slicing pepperoni, chopped
- ¼ pound deli-sliced provolone cheese, chopped
- 3 tablespoons red wine vinegar (eyeball it)
- ½ pound fresh mozzarella or fresh smoked mozzarella, diced
- 2 vine-ripe tomatoes, seeded and diced
- 1 cup basil leaves, torn or shredded

Preheat a grill pan or large nonstick skillet over medium-high or prepare an outdoor grill.

Place the meat in a bowl and season with salt and pepper. Add the egg yolk, cheese, tomato paste, parsley, garlic, and hot red pepper flakes. Mix the meat and form 12 large meatballs, 2 to 2½ inches each. Flatten the meatballs and form patties. Drizzle the patties with EVOO and add them to the hot pan or grill. Cook for 3 minutes on each side. Hold the cooked patties on a plate under foil.

On a large platter or in a salad bowl, combine the romaine with the quartered artichoke hearts, roasted red pepper, hot peppers, olives, celery, salami, and provolone. Toss the salad with vinegar first, about 3 tablespoons, then toss with EVOO—up to ¼ cup to your taste. (Just eyeball the amounts.) Season the salad with salt and pepper to taste. Scatter the chopped mozzarella, tomatoes, and basil across the salad. Arrange the cooked mini meatball burgers on top of the arranged antipasto salad.

TIDBIT

When dressing an oil and vinegar salad, put the acid on first, then the oil. If you add the EVOO first, the oil keeps the acid from getting to the greens.

Mini Cheeseburger Salad with Yellow Mustard Vinaigrette

There are many flavors of sharp Cheddar out in today's markets to choose from, so go plain or go wild! Among the choices out there in sharp Cheddars: five-peppercorn, smoked, dill, garlic and herb, roasted garlic, horseradish, chipotle, habanero, jalapeño—on and on!

4 SERVINGS, 3 MINI BURGERS EACH

- 2 pounds ground sirloin
- ½ cup finely chopped white or yellow onion (1 small onion)
- 2 tablespoons Worcestershire sauce
- 1 rounded tablespoon grill seasoning, such as McCormick's Montreal Steak Seasoning, or coarse salt and freshly ground black pepper
  Extra-virgin olive oil (EVOO), for drizzling
  12-ounce brick of sharp Cheddar cheese, such as Cabot brand or Cracker Barrel brand, any flavor you like
- 3 romaine lettuce hearts
- 1 cup sliced pickles, drained (choose from sweet, half-sour, or dill varieties)
- 1 cup cherry or grape tomatoes, halved

DRESSING

- 3 tablespoons yellow mustard, such as French's brand
- 2 tablespoons apple cider vinegar
- ½ cup extra-virgin olive oil (EVOO) (eyeball it)
- 2 to 3 tablespoons finely chopped fresh chives
- 3 tablespoons drained salad pimientos, or ¼ red bell pepper, finely chopped

Preheat a grill pan or a large nonstick skillet over medium-high heat or preheat an outdoor grill.

Combine the meat with the onion, Worcestershire, and steak seasoning or salt and pepper. Form 12 large meatballs. Flatten the balls into small patties. Drizzle the formed mini patties with EVOO to keep them from sticking to the cooking surface.

Slice the brick of cheese into ¼-inch pieces. Grill or panfry the mini burgers for 3 minutes on each side, then add the cheese to melt over the burgers, closing the lid of your grill to melt the cheese or tenting the mini cheeseburgers loosely with foil.

Coarsely chop the romaine and combine with the sliced pickles and halved tomatoes. Whisk together the mustard and vinegar, then stream in the EVOO. Add the chives and pimientos to the dressing and stir to combine.

Arrange the mini cheeseburgers on the salad and drizzle the yellow mustard dressing over the completed dish.

Feta-Studded Lamb Patties with Chunky Fresh Veggies

4 SERVINGS

1½ pounds ground lamb
  2 tablespoons Dijon mustard
  2 garlic cloves, finely chopped
     A handful of fresh flat-leaf parsley, chopped
     Salt and freshly ground black pepper
  ¼ pound feta cheese, cut into ¼-inch dice
  3 tablespoons extra-virgin olive oil (EVOO), divided
  2 vine-ripe tomatoes, each cut into 8 wedges
  ¼ cup pitted kalamata olives, roughly chopped
  4 cups baby spinach
 15 leaves of fresh mint, chopped
  1 can (15 ounces) chickpeas, drained, rinsed, and dried
  ½ English (seedless) cucumber (the one wrapped in plastic), cut in half lengthwise, then sliced into half-moons
  ½ tablespoon dried oregano
     Juice of 2 lemons
  2 pita flat breads, warmed and cut in half

continued ....➤

In a large bowl combine the lamb, Dijon mustard, garlic, 2 tablespoons of the chopped parsley, salt, and pepper and mix until combined. Add the feta cubes and fold the meat over itself a few times, trying not to break up the cubes of cheese too much. Once the feta cubes look evenly distributed, divide the meat into 4 equal portions. Form 4 patties about 1 inch thick. Season the outside of the patties with a little more pepper.

Preheat a large nonstick skillet over medium-high heat with 2 tablespoons of the EVOO (twice around the pan). Add the patties and cook for 3 or 4 minutes on each side for medium doneness or until your desired doneness. Hold the cooked patties on a plate under foil.

While the patties are cooking, put together the chunky fresh veggies: In a salad bowl combine the tomatoes, olives, spinach, mint, the remaining parsley, the chickpeas, cucumbers, oregano, lemon juice, the remaining tablespoon of EVOO, salt, and pepper. Toss to combine and coat.

Serve each patty on top of a portion of the chunky fresh veggies. Pass warm pita pieces at the table.

Haricots Frites

Why should potatoes have all the fun? These cute little French green beans are a lower-carb, lower-fat alternative to *pommes frites*, also known as: a pile of fries. Pair these with any of the Burgers, No Buns.

4 REGULAR SERVINGS OR 2 SUPERSIZED SERVINGS

     Salt
1¼ pounds (4 large handfuls) haricots verts (thin green beans), trimmed
  2 tablespoons light-colored oil, such as vegetable oil or peanut oil
  2 tablespoons sesame seeds

Bring 2 inches water to a boil in a large skillet. Salt the water once it comes to a boil. Blanch the haricots verts in the boiling water for 2 minutes, then drain and run under cold water to cool. Pat the beans dry on paper towels.

Dry the skillet as well and return it to the heat over high flame. Add oil to coat the bottom of the pan. Add the beans to the hot oil and stir-fry using tongs to move and toss the beans until they are charred and very hot, 3 to 4 minutes. Sprinkle the beans with the sesame seeds and cook for 30 seconds more, to both toast the seeds and distribute them. Pile the fried beans onto a serving plate and sprinkle with salt to taste.

Lamb Patties with Fattoush Salad

4 SERVINGS, 3 MINI PATTIES EACH

1½ pounds ground lamb

¼ cup finely chopped white or yellow onion (1 small onion)

1 teaspoon ground allspice (⅓ palmful)

1 tablespoon ground cumin (a palmful)

¼ teaspoon cinnamon (a couple of generous pinches)

2 tablespoons tomato paste

Several drops of hot sauce, such as Tabasco

Salt and freshly ground black pepper

3 tablespoons pine nuts, finely chopped

2 lemons, one zested and both juiced

Extra-virgin olive oil (EVOO) for drizzling, plus 3 to 4 tablespoons

¼ cup fresh mint (a handful of leaves), chopped

¼ cup fresh cilantro (a handful of leaves), chopped

½ cup fresh flat-leaf parsley (a couple of handfuls), coarsely chopped

1 romaine lettuce heart, chopped

2 cups arugula leaves (look in the bulk produce bins), chopped

2 vine-ripe tomatoes, seeded and chopped

3 or 4 radishes, sliced

4 scallions, thinly sliced on an angle

⅓ English (seedless) cucumber (the one wrapped in plastic), chopped

1 small bell pepper, any color, cored, seeded, and chopped

Heat a grill pan, large skillet, or outdoor grill over medium-high heat. In a large bowl combine the lamb with the onion, spices, tomato paste, hot sauce, salt and pepper, pine nuts, and lemon zest. Form 12 2- to 2½-inch balls. Flatten the balls into patties and drizzle with EVOO. Grill the patties for 2 to 3 minutes on each side. Hold the cooked patties on a plate under foil.

In a large, shallow platter mix the mint, cilantro, parsley, romaine, and arugula with the tomatoes, radishes, scallions, cucumbers, and bell pepper. Dress the salad with lemon juice and salt, toss, then dress with EVOO to taste. Top the salad with lamb patties and serve.

Gyro Burgers with Greek Salad

4 SERVINGS, 2 SMALL BURGERS EACH

1½ pounds ground chicken or ground lamb
 1 cup full-fat plain yogurt
    A handful of fresh flat-leaf parsley, chopped
 2 garlic cloves, finely chopped
 1 tablespoon ground cumin (a palmful)
1½ teaspoons dried oregano (half a palmful)
1½ teaspoons sweet paprika (half a palmful)
 1 tablespoon grill seasoning (a palmful; such as McCormick's
    Montreal Steak Seasoning)
    Extra-virgin olive oil (EVOO) for drizzling, plus about 3 tablespoons for dressing
 1 English (seedless) cucumber, diced into bite-size pieces
 1 red or green bell pepper, cored, seeded, and diced into bite-size pieces
 4 celery ribs with leafy greens intact, chopped
 ½ large red onion, chopped
 2 vine-ripe tomatoes, seeded and diced
 ½ pound feta, crumbled
 ½ cup pitted kalamata olives, coarsely chopped
 6 peperoncini (pickled hot, light green peppers), chopped
    Juice of 2 lemons
    Several drops of hot sauce, such as Tabasco
    Coarse salt
    Pita bread, warmed and cut in half

Preheat a grill pan, large nonstick skillet, or outdoor grill to medium-high heat.

In a large bowl combine the ground meat with the yogurt, parsley, garlic, spices, and seasonings. Form 8 thin 3-inch patties. Drizzle the patties with EVOO and cook for 3 minutes on each side in 2 batches. Hold the cooked patties on a plate under foil.

In a large, shallow serving bowl combine the cucumber, bell pepper, celery, red onion, tomatoes, feta, olives, and peperoncini. Dress the salad with lemon juice, hot sauce, and salt. Toss, add about 3 tablespoons EVOO, and toss again. Taste to adjust seasonings. Top the salad with the patties and serve with pita bread.

FAJITA BURGERS

Serve the Seared Peppers and Onions (page 46) with any or all of these Fajita Burgers. They're hot! Wrap the pepper and onion topping in a warm, soft tortilla with a burger, or pile a quarter of the mixture on each plate and garnish with a little cilantro. Top with a burger of your choice.

Beef Fajita Burgers

4 BURGERS

- 2 pounds ground sirloin
- 2 tablespoons Worcestershire sauce (eyeball it)
- 2 tablespoons chili powder (a palmful)
- 1½ teaspoons ground cumin (half a palmful)
- 2 to 3 tablespoons fresh thyme leaves (several sprigs)
  Several drops of hot sauce, such as Tabasco
- 2 tablespoons grill seasoning (such as McCormick's Montreal Steak Seasoning)
  Extra-virgin olive oil (EVOO), for drizzling
- 1 package of large flour tortillas, warmed and passed at the table

Heat a grill pan or large skillet over medium-high heat.

In a large bowl combine the meat, Worcestershire, spices, thyme, hot sauce, and grill seasoning. Score and divide the meat into 4 sections and make 4 large patties, 1 inch thick. Drizzle EVOO on the patties. Cook the patties for 5 or 6 minutes on each side or until desired doneness.

Shrimp Fajita Burgers

4 BURGERS

1½ pounds raw medium shrimp, shelled and deveined, tails removed
  1 tablespoon chili powder (half a palmful)
  1 tablespoon Old Bay or other seafood seasoning (half a palmful)
     Several drops of hot sauce, such as Tabasco
  2 to 3 tablespoons fresh thyme leaves
  1 teaspoon coarse black pepper
     Zest and juice of 1 lemon
     A handful of fresh flat-leaf parsley leaves
  1 celery rib, chopped
  1 garlic clove, smashed out of its skin
  2 tablespoons extra-virgin olive oil (EVOO) (twice around)
  1 package of large flour tortillas, warmed and passed at the table

Heat a large skillet over medium-high heat.

Place half of the shrimp in a food processor bowl with the chili powder, Old Bay seasoning, hot sauce, thyme leaves, black pepper, lemon zest and juice, parsley, celery, and garlic. Process the mixture for 1 minute to combine. Transfer the mixture to a bowl. Chop the remaining shrimp and fold into the ground shrimp. Get a large metal ice cream scoop and place it in the bowl. Add the EVOO to the skillet. Mound a quarter of the shrimp mixture into the scoop at a time and transfer it to the hot pan. Use a fish spatula to gently press the shrimp mixture into patties and fry them for 5 minutes on each side or until firm and opaque.

Chicken Fajita Burgers

4 BURGERS

- 2 pounds ground chicken
- 2 tablespoons chipotle (smoky flavor) chili powder (a palmful)
- 2 to 3 tablespoons chopped fresh cilantro
  Several drops of hot sauce, such as Tabasco
- 2 tablespoons grill seasoning, such as McCormick's Montreal Steak Seasoning
  Extra-virgin olive oil (EVOO), for drizzling
- 1 package of large flour tortillas, warmed and passed at the table

Heat a grill pan or large skillet over medium-high heat.

In a large bowl combine the chicken, chipotle powder, cilantro, hot sauce, and grill seasoning. Score and divide the meat into 4 sections and form 4 big patties, 1 inch thick. Drizzle the patties with EVOO and cook for 6 minutes on each side or until the meat is firm and cooked through.

Seared Peppers and Onions

4 SERVINGS

- 1 tablespoon extra-virgin olive oil (EVOO) (once around the pan)
- 2 large red or green bell peppers, cored, seeded, and thinly sliced lengthwise
- 1 large yellow onion, thinly sliced lengthwise
- 2 garlic cloves, smashed out of their skin and chopped
- 1 jalapeño or serrano chili, seeded and chopped
- 1 cup tomatillo or green chili salsa, your choice
- 2 tablespoons chopped fresh cilantro, for garnish

Heat a large skillet over high heat. Add the EVOO and the peppers and onions. Stir-fry the veggies, tossing them with tongs to sear them at the edges. Add the garlic and the jalapeño or serrano chili. Toss and turn the mixture for about 3 minutes, then add your salsa of choice and toss a minute longer.

Turkey Cacciatore Burgers on Portobello "Buns"

4 SERVINGS

1⅓ pounds ground turkey breast (the average weight of 1 package)
   Salt and freshly ground black pepper
6 crimini mushrooms (baby portobellos), stemmed and finely chopped
½ red bell pepper, cored, seeded, and chopped
½ yellow onion, finely chopped
2 garlic cloves, smashed out of their skin and finely chopped
3 tablespoons tomato paste
1 tablespoon Worcestershire sauce
1 teaspoon crushed hot red pepper flakes
½ cup grated Parmigiano-Reggiano or Romano cheese (a couple of handfuls)
   A handful of fresh flat-leaf parsley, chopped
   Extra-virgin olive oil (EVOO), for drizzling
4 large portobello mushroom caps, stems discarded
   Coarse salt and coarse black pepper
2 cups arugula leaves, coarsely chopped
½ pound fresh mozzarella or fresh smoked mozzarella, thinly sliced

Preheat the oven to 450°F. Heat a large nonstick skillet over medium-high heat.

In a large bowl combine the meat with salt and pepper, the crimini mushrooms, bell pepper, onion, garlic, tomato paste, Worcestershire, crushed red pepper flakes, cheese, and parsley. Score and divide the meat into 4 portions. Form each portion into a large patty, 1 inch thick. Drizzle EVOO on top of the patties, then fry for 5 or 6 minutes on each side in the hot skillet. Hold the cooked patties on a plate under foil.

continued ·······················➤

Place the portobello caps on a small baking sheet gill side up and drizzle EVOO on them. Roast the caps for 12 minutes. Remove them from the oven and season them with coarse salt and pepper. Turn the oven off. Top each cap with about ½ cup arugula and a burger. Layer each burger with mozzarella and place back in the still-warm oven for about 1 minute to melt the cheese. Transfer the burgers on "bun" bottoms to plates and serve.

Cubano Pork Burgers and Sweet Orange Warm Slaw

Cubanos are traditionally served on a sweet roll. The orange juice and honey are used to hit that sweet note here.

4 SERVINGS

- 1¾ pounds ground pork
- 4 garlic cloves, chopped
- Zest and juice of 2 navel oranges
- 1 tablespoon ground cumin (a palmful)
- 1½ teaspoons coriander (half a palmful)
- 3 tablespoons yellow mustard, such as French's brand
- Several drops of hot sauce, such as Tabasco
- Salt and freshly ground black pepper
- ¼ cup vegetable oil
- 12 pickle slices, dill, garlic, or sour
- 4 deli slices baked or boiled ham
- 4 deli slices Swiss cheese
- 1 small red onion, thinly sliced
- ¼ cup red wine vinegar
- 1 tablespoon honey (a good drizzle)
- 1 16-ounce sack of coleslaw mix (found on the produce aisle)
- 1 small red bell pepper, seeded and thinly sliced
- A handful of fresh cilantro leaves, chopped
- A handful of fresh flat-leaf parsley leaves, chopped
- 4 Portuguese rolls, split

In a bowl combine the ground pork, half of the chopped garlic, half of the orange zest, the cumin, coriander, mustard, hot sauce, salt, and pepper. Score the meat into 4 sections and then form 4 large patties about 1 inch thick.

Preheat a medium skillet with 2 tablespoons of the vegetable oil (twice around the pan), over medium-high heat. Add the patties to the hot skillet and cook on the first side for 6 minutes. Flip and top each patty with three pickles, a slice of ham, and a slice of Swiss. Cook the patties for another 5 to 6 minutes. Place a foil tent over the pan for the last 2 minutes or so to ensure that the cheese melts and the fixings heat up.

While the patties are cooking, make the sweet orange warm slaw. Preheat a large skillet with the remaining veg oil. Add the remaining garlic and the sliced onion to the hot oil and cook for 1 minute. Add the remaining orange zest, the orange juice, red wine vinegar, and honey. Continue cooking the dressing for 1 minute. Turn the heat off and add the coleslaw mix, red bell pepper, cilantro, parsley, and salt and pepper, tossing to coat in the warm dressing.

Serve your Cubano burgers on Portuguese rolls with the sweet orange warm slaw both on top of the burger and alongside.

Ginger–Garlic Tuna Burgers on Cucumber Salad with Salted Edamame

4 SERVINGS

- 1¾ to 2 pounds **ahi tuna**, cut into cubes
- 3-inch piece fresh **gingerroot**, peeled and grated
- 4 **garlic** cloves, finely chopped
- 3 to 4 tablespoons **tamari** (dark aged soy sauce) (eyeball it)
- 2 teaspoons **coarse black pepper**
- 2 **scallions**, finely chopped
- 2 tablespoons finely chopped fresh **cilantro**
- **Vegetable oil**, for drizzling, plus some for the salad
- 1 **romaine lettuce** heart, chopped
- 2 cups fresh **bean sprouts** or pea shoots
- ½ **English (seedless) cucumber** (the one wrapped in plastic), cut into ¼-inch dice
- Juice and zest of 1 **lime**
- **Coarse salt**
- 1 pound **edamame** (soybeans in pods available in freezer section of market)

Heat a grill pan or large skillet over high heat.

Place the fish in a food processor and pulse until the fish is the consistency of ground beef. Transfer the ground ahi to a bowl and mix with the ginger, garlic, tamari, black pepper, scallions, and cilantro. Form 4 equal patties and drizzle them with vegetable oil. Place the tuna burgers in a screaming hot pan and cook for 1 minute on each side for very rare, 2 minutes on each side for medium rare, 3 to 4 minutes on each side to cook through. Hold the cooked patties on a plate under foil.

In a medium bowl combine the lettuce, sprouts, and cucumber. Dress the salad with the lime zest and juice, salt, and vegetable oil to your taste.

Place the edamame in a microwave bowl and cover with plastic wrap. Pop a small hole in the top of the wrap and microwave on High for 5 minutes. When the time is up, sprinkle the edamame with 2 teaspoons of coarse salt and toss.

Pile the salad up equally onto 4 plates. Top the salad with tuna patties. Pile the edamame alongside the burgers. To enjoy the edamame, shimmy the soybeans free from their pods in your mouth. Who misses fries? (Well, okay, they're good too, but soybeans are actually good for you as well!)

Danish Burgers with Herb Caper Sauce and a Mod Salad

4 SERVINGS

- 2 pounds ground chicken
- 1 tablespoon poultry seasoning (a palmful)
- 2 shallots, finely chopped
- 2 tablespoons Dijon mustard
- 5 button mushrooms, stems discarded, finely chopped
- ¼ pound Havarti with dill cheese, cut into ¼-inch dice
  Salt and freshly ground black pepper
  Extra-virgin olive oil (EVOO), for drizzling, plus a couple tablespoons for the salad
- ½ cup mayonnaise or sour cream
- 2 to 3 tablespoons fresh dill, chopped or snipped with kitchen scissors
- 2 tablespoons capers, drained, then run your knife through them once
- 1 English (seedless) cucumber (the one wrapped in plastic), cut in half lengthwise, then sliced into half-moons
- 1 small red onion, sliced
- 3 plum tomatoes, seeded and thinly sliced
  1-pound sack of washed baby spinach
- 2 to 3 tablespoons white wine vinegar
- 4 crusty poppyseed rolls

continued ....➤

2 large radishes, thinly sliced
1 sack of gourmet potato chips, such as Terra Chips Onion and Herb Yukon Gold, or Blue Potato Chips

In a bowl, thoroughly combine the ground chicken, poultry seasoning, shallots, Dijon mustard, mushrooms, Havarti, salt, and pepper. Score the meat with your hand into 4 equal portions. Form each portion into a large 1-inch-thick patty.

Preheat a nonstick skillet over medium-high heat. Drizzle EVOO over the patties and place them in the hot skillet. Cook for 6 minutes per side until the patties are firm to the touch and cooked through.

While the burgers are cooking prepare the herb caper sauce and mod salad. In a small bowl combine the mayonnaise or sour cream, dill, and capers. Set aside. In a salad bowl combine the cucumbers, red onion, plum tomatoes, and three quarters of the baby spinach. Dress the salad with white wine vinegar, salt, and pepper, then drizzle with a couple tablespoons of EVOO to coat the salad lightly and evenly. Toss to combine and adjust the salt and pepper to your taste.

Split the rolls. Place the burgers on the bun bottoms. Top with sliced radishes, the remaining baby spinach, and a heaping spoonful of the herb-caper dressing slathered across the bun tops. Add the remaining sauce to the salad and toss for a creamy finish. Fancy chips finish the plate.

TIDBIT

The colder the semisoft Havarti with dill cheese is, the easier it will be to dice. Pop the cheese in the freezer while you prep everything else. Because of the fat content of the cheese, just 10 minutes in a deep freeze makes the dicing a real breeze!

Sausage Patty Melt

Instead of two slices of bread and one patty, this lower-carb patty melt has two patties sandwiching cheese, peppers, and onions. Skip lunch. This one's a gut-buster!

4 SERVINGS

  Extra-virgin olive oil (EVOO), for drizzling, plus 1 tablespoon (once around the pan)
4 Italian hot sausage patties
4 Italian sweet sausage patties
1 cubanelle pepper (long, light green, fresh Italian pepper), seeded and sliced
1 red bell pepper, cored, seeded, and thinly sliced
1 medium onion, thinly sliced
2 garlic cloves, smashed out of their skin
1 teaspoon crushed hot red pepper flakes
  Salt
8 deli slices provolone cheese

Heat a large nonstick skillet or grill pan for the patties, another medium skillet for the peppers and onions, over medium-high heat.

Drizzle the nonstick pan or grill pan with EVOO and fry the sausage patties in 2 batches, 2 hot and 2 sweet at a time. The patties cook in 5 to 6 minutes per side, so you can make 2 batches in less than 30 minutes.

While the sausages cook, add 1 tablespoon EVOO to the second skillet and fry up the peppers, onion, and garlic for 6 to 7 minutes, until tender but still full of color and a little crunch. Season the veggies with the red pepper flakes and salt to taste.

To assemble, pile some peppers and onions on a sweet sausage patty. Top with 2 slices of the provolone and a hot sausage patty. Press to set. Hold the patties under a foil tent for 1 minute so the cheese melts and the 2 patties and veggies all stick together.

Hungarian Turkey Burgers Studded with Smoked Gouda

4 SERVINGS

1⅓ pounds ground turkey (the average weight of 1 package)
1 small yellow onion, finely chopped
½ red bell pepper, cored, seeded, and finely chopped
A handful of fresh flat-leaf parsley, chopped
Several drops of Worcestershire sauce
1 tablespoon smoked paprika (a palmful)
Salt and freshly ground black pepper
⅓ pound smoked Gouda cheese, cut into ¼-inch dice
Extra-virgin olive oil (EVOO), for drizzling
1 cup watercress, finely chopped
1 small shallot, minced
1 cup sour cream
8 red leaf lettuce leaves
4 slices pumpernickel bread
4 celery ribs, cut into sticks
8 radishes, trimmeg

Heat a large nonstick skillet or grill pan over medium-high heat. In a large bowl mix the turkey with the onion, bell pepper, parsley, Worcestershire, smoked paprika, salt, and pepper. Fold in the chopped smoked Gouda. Score the meat with your hand into 4 sections. Form each section into a large patty 1 inch thick. Drizzle the patties with EVOO and cook for 6 minutes on each side, until cooked through.

While the burgers cook, mix the watercress, shallot, and sour cream in a small bowl. Season the thick sauce with salt to taste.

To serve, place 2 lettuce leaves on each slice of bread. Top with a burger. Top burgers with some sauce and serve with a few celery sticks and radishes on the side for munching (they're good with the sauce, too).

Grilled Surf and Turf: Sirloin Burgers on Bed of Lettuce with Grilled Shrimp and Horseradish Chili Sauce

This burger and the side that follows are fancy enough to entertain with and much more affordable than steaks and lobster for your crew!

4 SERVINGS

1½ pounds ground sirloin
1 large shallot, finely chopped
2 tablespoons fresh thyme leaves, chopped
1 tablespoon Worcestershire sauce
1 teaspoon smoked Hungarian paprika or 2 teaspoons ground cumin (eyeball it)
2 teaspoons grill seasoning, such as McCormick's Montreal Steak Seasoning, or coarse salt and coarse black pepper
Extra-virgin olive oil (EVOO), for drizzling
8 raw jumbo shrimp, peeled and deveined
1 tablespoon chopped fresh flat-leaf parsley
1 lemon, zested and then cut into wedges
2 garlic cloves, finely chopped
½ head iceberg lettuce, cored and quartered
2 rounded tablespoons prepared horseradish
1 cup bottled chili sauce
4 slices of toasted white or wheat bread

Preheat a grill pan or outdoor grill to high.

In a large bowl combine the beef, shallot, thyme, Worcestershire, smoked paprika or cumin, and grill seasoning. Divide the meat into 4 portions and form large patties about 1¼ inches thick.

continued ....➤

Coat the beef patties with a drizzle of EVOO. Cook for 3 to 4 minutes on each side for medium rare, 6 minutes per side for medium well to well-done.

Cut the shrimp along the deveining line and "butterfly" them open a little. Be careful not to cut all the way through the shrimp and to leave the tails intact. Place the shrimp in a shallow dish and coat in EVOO. Sprinkle with the grill seasoning or salt and pepper. Add the parsley, lemon zest, and garlic and turn the shrimp to coat evenly in flavorings. Grill the shrimp alongside the meat patties for 2 to 3 minutes on each side, until heads curl toward tails and the shrimp are pink.

While the meat and shrimp cook, arrange 4 beds of cut iceberg lettuce on a platter and combine the horseradish with chili sauce in a small bowl. To serve, place the burgers on toast with lettuce "buns" as tops and dot with sauce, then top with 2 grilled shrimp. Pass the remaining sauce and the lemon wedges at the table. Serve with Bacon-Wrapped Asparagus Bundles (page 57).

Bacon-Wrapped Asparagus Bundles

These bundles can be easily prepared on an outdoor grill or in a hot oven.

4 SERVINGS

- 1 to 1¼ pounds asparagus tips, 4 to 5 inches long
  Extra-virgin olive oil (EVOO), for drizzling
  Salt and freshly ground black pepper
- 4 slices center-cut bacon or pancetta
  Chopped fresh chives or scallions, for garnish (optional)

Preheat the oven, if using, to 400°F. or preheat an outdoor grill.

Lightly coat the asparagus spears in EVOO. Season the asparagus with salt and pepper. Take a quick count of the spear tips. Divide the total number by four. Gather that number of spears and use a slice of bacon to wrap the bundle and secure the spears together. Repeat with the remaining ingredients.

To grill, place the bundles on the hot grill and cover. Cook for 10 to 12 minutes over indirect heat until the bacon is crisp and the asparagus bundles are tender.

For oven preparation, place the bundles on a slotted broiler pan. Bake for 12 minutes, or until the bacon is crisp and the asparagus bundles are tender.

Sprinkle with the chopped chives and serve.

Cheddar-Studded Chili Turkey Burgers with Cilantro Cream and South of the Border Iceberg

4 SERVINGS

1⅓ pounds ground turkey breast (the average weight of 1 package)
1 medium red onion, half finely chopped, half diced
¼ pound sharp Cheddar cheese, cut into ¼-inch dice
1 rounded tablespoon chili powder (a healthy palmful)
2 teaspoons ground cumin (⅔ palmful)
1 jalapeño or serrano chili, seeded and finely chopped
2 garlic cloves, chopped
  Salt and freshly ground black pepper
3 tablespoons extra-virgin olive oil (EVOO), plus some for drizzling
½ cup sour cream
  A handful of fresh cilantro leaves, chopped
½ head iceberg lettuce, chopped
1 ripe mango, peeled and diced
1 small red bell pepper, cored, seeded, and cut into thin strips
1 ripe Hass avocado
2 limes
4 Corn Toasties (corn toaster cakes), any brand, toasted

Preheat a large nonstick skillet, indoor grill pan, or tabletop grill to medium-high heat.

In a medium bowl combine the ground turkey, the finely chopped onion, the Cheddar, chili powder, cumin, jalapeño, garlic, salt, and pepper. Score the meat with the side of your hand to separate into 4 equal amounts. Form into 4 large patties no more than 1 inch thick. Drizzle EVOO on the patties and place them in the hot skillet or on the hot grill. Cook for 5 to 6 minutes on each side, or until the turkey is cooked through.

While the burgers are cooking, prepare the rest of the meal. For the cilantro cream, in a small bowl combine the sour cream, chopped cilantro, and salt and pepper to taste.

Next, in a salad bowl combine the chopped iceberg, mango, red bell pepper, and the diced onion. Cut all around the circumference of the ripe avocado, lengthwise and down to the pit. Twist and separate the halved fruit. Remove the pit with a spoon, then scoop the flesh out in one piece from both halves. Chop the avocado into bite-size pieces and add them to the salad. Squeeze the juice of 2 limes over the salad and drizzle with about 3 tablespoons of EVOO, season with salt and pepper, and toss to coat.

Serve the Cheddar-studded turkey burgers topped with a little of the cilantro cream on toaster cakes and a mound of the iceberg salad alongside.

TIDBIT

Get your juices flowing! To get lots of juice from your lemons and limes, heat them in a microwave for 10 seconds on High before you juice them. When you are juicing lemons, remember to hold them cut side up when you squeeze them so the pits remain with the lemon and not in your recipe.

Chicken Kiev Burgers and Russian-Style Slaw Salad

The herbed butter in the center of the burger adds great flavor and tons of moisture and is a good-time, exploding centerpiece to this fast and simple meal.

4 SERVINGS

¼ cup fresh flat-leaf parsley, chopped

2 tablespoons chopped fresh chives

1 tablespoon fresh thyme leaves, chopped (a few sprigs, stripped)

4 tablespoon-size tabs of cold butter (½ stick cut in 4 thick slices)

2 pounds ground chicken

3 tablespoons Worcestershire sauce

3 tablespoons Dijon mustard, divided

Salt and freshly ground black pepper

Extra-virgin olive oil (EVOO), for drizzling

4 rounded tablespoons sour cream

Juice of 1 lemon

4 to 5 tablespoons chopped fresh dill

1 tablespoon prepared horseradish

8 radishes, sliced

½ small red onion, thinly sliced

2 cups shredded carrots (on the produce aisle)

1 English (seedless) cucumber (the one wrapped in plastic), cut in half lengthwise, then thinly sliced into half-moons

3 celery ribs, thinly sliced

2 cups coleslaw mix (on the produce aisle)

4 slices of rye bread or marble rye, toasted

Preheat a large nonstick skillet, indoor grill pan, or tabletop grill to medium-high heat.

On your cutting board, combine 2 tablespoons of the chopped parsley, the chopped chives, and the chopped thyme. Dip the tabs of cold butter into the herbs one at a time, pressing the herbs into the butter to coat them completely.

In a medium bowl combine the ground chicken, Worcestershire sauce, 2 tablespoons of the mustard, salt, and pepper. Form the mixture into 4 large patties no more than 1 inch thick. Nest 1 herb-coated cold butter tab into the center of each patty and gently form the patty around the butter. Drizzle EVOO over the patties and place them in a hot skillet or on a hot grill. Cook for 5 to 6 minutes on each side.

While the burgers are cooking, in a mixing bowl thoroughly combine the sour cream, lemon juice, dill, horseradish, and the remaining tablespoon of mustard. Add the radishes, red onion, carrots, cucumber, celery, coleslaw mix, the remaining 2 tablespoons of chopped parsley, and salt and pepper to taste. Toss to combine. Serve the Kiev burgers open-faced on a slice of toast with the salad alongside.

CHAPTER 3

TAKE A DIP!

Metro-Retro fondues make dinner more fun than a pile of carbs!

Each fondue recipe has suggestions for dippers, but each recipe is
terrific with any meat, sausage, pickle, or blanched vegetable
that you like, so get creative!

Smoked Gouda Fondue with Bacon and Almonds

4 SERVINGS

- 6 slices thick-cut bacon
- 8 ounces Gruyère cheese, shredded
- 1/3 pound (about 6 ounces) smoked Gouda, shredded
- 1 rounded tablespoon flour
- 1 large garlic clove, smashed out of its skin
- 3/4 cup dry white wine
- 2 teaspoons fresh lemon juice
- 1/2 cup smoked almonds (I like Diamond brand), coarsely chopped

SERVE WITH . . .

Blanched bite-size pieces of cauliflower, white asparagus, parsnip
Seared cubes of kielbasa
Cornichon pickles
Red pears, slightly underripe

Broil or fry the bacon until crisp. Drain, cool, and chop.

Combine the cheeses in a bowl with the flour. Rub the inside of a small pot with the smashed garlic, then discard the garlic. Add the wine and lemon juice to the pot and bring up to a bubble over medium heat. Reduce the heat to simmer and add the cheese mixture in handfuls. Stir constantly in a figure-eight pattern with a wooden spoon, melting the cheese in batches. Transfer the fondue to a fondue pot and top with chopped bacon and smoked nuts.

German Cheddar and Beer Fondue

- 10 ounces (2½ cups) shredded sharp Cheddar cheese (on the dairy aisle)
- 4 to 6 ounces Gruyère cheese, shredded (1 to 1½ cups)
- 1 rounded tablespoon flour
- 1 cup German lager
- 2 tablespoons spicy brown mustard
    A few drops of hot sauce, such as Tabasco
    A few drops of Worcestershire sauce

SERVE WITH . . .

    Cubed or thick-sliced and browned wursts: knack or brat
    Mini party franks, such as Boar's Head brand
    Blanched cauliflower and broccoli florets

In a bowl combine the cheeses with the flour. Add the beer to a small pot and bring up to a bubble over medium heat. Reduce the heat to simmer and add the cheese mixture in handfuls. Stir constantly in a figure-eight pattern with a wooden spoon, melting the cheese in batches. When the cheese has been incorporated fully, stir in the mustard, hot sauce, and Worcestershire sauce. Transfer the fondue to a fondue pot and serve.

Spanish Cheese and Olive Fondue

4 SERVINGS

- 8 ounces manchego cheese, shredded
- 8 ounces Gruyère cheese, shredded
- 1 rounded tablespoon flour
- 1 large garlic clove, crushed out of its skin
- 1¼ cups dry white wine
- 1 teaspoon sweet paprika
  A few drops of Tabasco or other hot sauce
- ¼ cup coarsely chopped large pitted good-quality green olives
- 3 tablespoons chopped pimientos

SERVE WITH . . .

Pan-seared chunks of chorizo sausage
Grilled chicken breasts, cut into bite-size cubes
Fresh bell pepper chunks

In a bowl combine the cheeses with the flour. Rub the inside of a small pot with the garlic, then discard the garlic. Add the wine to the pot and bring up to a bubble over medium heat. Reduce the heat to simmer and add the cheese mixture in handfuls. Stir constantly in a figure-eight pattern with a wooden spoon, melting the cheese in batches. When the cheese has been incorporated fully, stir in the paprika, hot sauce, olives, and pimientos. Transfer the fondue to a fondue pot and serve.

Italian Fonduta with Roasted Red Pepper

4 SERVINGS

- ⅓ pound, about 6 ounces Gruyère cheese, shredded
- ½ pound fresh mozzarella cheese or fresh smoked mozzarella cheese, shredded
- ¼ cup grated Parmigiano-Reggiano or Romano cheese (a handful)
- 1 rounded tablespoon flour
- 1 cup dry white wine
- 1 tablespoon fresh lemon juice
- 2 garlic cloves, minced
- ½ roasted red bell pepper, finely diced (about 3 tablespoons)

SERVE WITH . . .

Chunks of cooked Italian sweet and hot sausages
Cubed salami
Cubed cooked balsamic-marinated chicken breast, grilled or pan fried
Giardiniera Italian hot pickled vegetables, drained

In a bowl combine the cheeses with the flour. Add the wine to a small pot and bring up to a bubble over medium heat. Reduce the heat to simmer and add the lemon juice, then the cheese mixture in handfuls. Stir constantly in a figure-eight pattern with a wooden spoon, melting the cheese in batches. When the cheese has been incorporated fully, stir in the minced garlic and chopped roasted red pepper. Transfer the fondue to a fondue pot and serve.

Mexican Fondue

4 SERVINGS

- 8 ounces Pepper Jack cheese, shredded
- 4 ounces Gruyère cheese, shredded
- 4 ounces Cheddar cheese, shredded
- 1 tablespoon cornstarch
- 1 cup Mexican beer
- 2 teaspoons hot sauce, such as Tabasco
- Zest of 1 lime plus 1 tablespoon fresh lime juice
- 3 tablespoons canned green chili peppers, finely chopped
- 3 tablespoons green salad olives with pimientos, finely chopped
- 2 tablespoons chopped fresh cilantro, for garnish (optional)

SERVE WITH . . .

Grilled chicken or steak, cubed
Grilled, chopped linguiça sausage
Sliced zucchini
Chunks of bell peppers

In a small bowl combine the cheeses and cornstarch. Add the beer to a small pot and bring up to a bubble over medium heat. Reduce the heat to simmer and add the hot sauce, lime zest and juice, then the cheese mixture in handfuls. Stir constantly in a figure-eight pattern with a wooden spoon, melting the cheese in batches. When the cheese has been incorporated fully, stir in the chili peppers and olives with pimientos. Transfer the fondue to a fondue pot and garnish with cilantro, if using, then serve.

Go Greek! Feta Fondue with Garlic and Mint

4 SERVINGS

- 2 tablespoons butter
- 2 garlic cloves, chopped
- 2 tablespoons flour
- 1½ cups milk
- 8 ounces Greek feta cheese, diced
- 2 tablespoons chopped fresh mint
- 2 tablespoons chopped fresh flat-leaf parsley
- 1 teaspoon coarse black pepper

SERVE WITH . . .

Small baked lamb, beef, or chicken meatballs

Greek sausage, grilled and cut into chunks

Cubed cooked lamb, beef, or chicken

Grilled shrimp

Cubed raw bell peppers, cucumbers, celery, or tomatoes

Heat a small pot over medium heat. Melt the butter in the pot, add the garlic, and sauté for 2 minutes. Add the flour and stir to combine with the butter and garlic. Cook the flour for 1 minute, then whisk in the milk and bring it up to a bubble. Add the feta and melt it into the milk. When the cheese has melted into the sauce, stir in the mint, parsley, and black pepper. Transfer the sauce to a fondue pot and serve.

Classic Swiss Fondue

4 SERVINGS

1 large garlic clove, crushed out of its skin
1¼ cups dry white wine
1 tablespoon fresh lemon juice
8 ounces Gruyère cheese, shredded
8 ounces Emmentaler cheese, shredded
1 tablespoon cornstarch
¼ cup kirschwasser (cherry brandy)
½ teaspoon freshly grated nutmeg
White pepper or cayenne

SERVE WITH . . .

Cubed ham
Marinated mushrooms or fresh whole sautéed button mushrooms
Blanched asparagus or white asparagus
Whole trimmed radishes
Small dill pickles or cornichons

Rub the inside of a small pot with the garlic, then discard the garlic. Add the wine to the pot and bring up to a bubble over medium heat. Reduce the heat to simmer and add the lemon juice, then the cheeses in handfuls. Stir constantly in a figure-eight pattern with a wooden spoon, melting the cheese in batches. When the cheese has been incorporated fully, stir the cornstarch into the brandy in a small bowl and then stir the brandy into the cheese. Season the fondue with the nutmeg and white or cayenne pepper, to taste. Transfer the fondue to a fondue pot and serve.

CHAPTER **4**

SALADS THAT STACK UP!

Perfect for lunch or dinner, these salads-turned-meals are stacked up with seafood, meats, and/or cheeses.

You'll not find a chef salad like any of these at the corner diner. The flavors in these salads stack up almost as high as the ingredients!

Korean Barbecued Flank Steak on Hot and Sour Slaw Salad

4 SERVINGS

- 1 tablespoon grill seasoning, such as McCormick's Montreal Steak Seasoning
- ¼ cup tamari (dark aged soy sauce)
- 2 tablespoons honey
- 2 teaspoons hot red pepper flakes
- 4 large garlic cloves, chopped
- 2 teaspoons dark sesame oil (eyeball it)
- 2 scallions, finely chopped
  Vegetable oil, for drizzling, plus 2 tablespoons (twice around the pan)
- 2 pounds flank steak
- 1 pound bok choy or napa cabbage, trimmed and shredded with a knife
- ½ red bell pepper, cored, seeded, and thinly sliced
  Salt
- 1 cup sauerkraut (it will taste like kim chee when combined with hot red pepper flakes)

In a shallow dish, combine the grill seasoning, tamari, 1 tablespoon of the honey, 1 teaspoon of the red pepper flakes, half of the chopped garlic, the sesame oil, scallions, and a drizzle of vegetable oil. Coat the flank steak in the mixture and let it stand for 10 minutes.

Preheat an indoor electric grill, a stovetop grill pan, or an outdoor grill to medium high. When the grill pan or grill is screaming hot, add the meat and cook for 5 minutes on each side for medium rare, 7 to 8 minutes on each side for medium well.

continued ....➤

Heat a large skillet over high heat. Add 2 tablespoons of the vegetable oil, the cabbage, and the bell pepper. Season with salt and stir-fry for 2 or 3 minutes. Add a drizzle of honey (the remaining tablespoon), the remaining red pepper flakes, and the remaining garlic and toss to combine with the cabbage. Add the sauerkraut and mix in, heating it through for 1 minute. Turn off the heat.

To serve, let the meat rest for 5 minutes for juices to redistribute. Thinly slice the meat on a heavy angle against the grain (the lines in the meat). Pile up the slaw, top with the sliced Korean steak, and serve.

Good Taste Menu

Lemon, Garlic, and Cilantro Baked Stuffed Tomatoes

Surf and Turf Salad

This is what I call a mixed menu: It appeals to low carbers and high carbers alike. Whether you carb it and your mate is watching it or you're low-carbing it and your friends and family are not, serve this menu and everyone will be happy and healthier for it. Cook up the Surf and Turf while the tomatoes are baking.

Lemon, Garlic, and Cilantro Baked Stuffed Tomatoes

This dish makes a perfect side for a simple grilled steak any time of year. With the Surf and Turf Salad it's a knockout!

4 SERVINGS

- 2 beefsteak tomatoes
  Salt and freshly ground black pepper
- 1 cup whole-milk ricotta cheese
  Zest of 1 large lemon (2 tablespoons)
- ¼ cup fresh cilantro leaves, chopped
- ¾ cup fresh flat-leaf parsley, chopped
- 2 garlic cloves, chopped
- 2 scallions, finely chopped
- ⅓ cup grated Parmigiano-Reggiano
- 1 egg yolk
  Extra-virgin olive oil (EVOO), for drizzling

Preheat the oven to 450°F.

For the baked stuffed tomatoes you will need to make 4 tomato cups out of your 2 tomatoes. To do so, cut a very thin slice off both ends of each of the tomatoes to create 4 flat bottoms. Then cut each tomato in half, across, making 4 tomato cups.

To create a cavity, use a melon-ball scoop to remove the seeds and guts from the wide, fleshy side of each tomato cup. You don't have to be too fussy about this. You are just trying to create enough room to hold the filling. When scooping, take some care not to rip through the bottoms of the cups. (If you do rip one, don't worry, it is not the end of the world, just keep moving forward. That tomato will just be tricky to transfer to the plate.) Season the inside of the tomato cavities with salt and pepper. Reserve the seasoned tomato cups while you make the filling.

continued ....➤

In a small mixing bowl combine the ricotta cheese, lemon zest, cilantro, parsley, garlic, scallions, and Parmigiano cheese, then season with salt and pepper. Taste the mixture. This is your last chance to adjust the seasoning. Once you're happy with the flavor, add the egg yolk and mix thoroughly. Divide the filling among the 4 tomato cups, pushing it into the cavity with a rubber spatula or spoon. Drizzle EVOO into a baking dish. Arrange the stuffed tomatoes in the dish and bake for 15 to 17 minutes, until lightly brown and cooked through.

Surf and Turf Salad

4 SERVINGS

2 large garlic cloves, minced

1-inch piece fresh gingerroot, peeled and minced or grated

3 tablespoons tamari (dark aged soy sauce)

1 teaspoon coriander ($\frac{1}{3}$ palmful)

2 teaspoons ground cumin ($\frac{1}{2}$ to $\frac{2}{3}$ palmful)

1 teaspoon turmeric ($\frac{1}{3}$ palmful)

$\frac{1}{2}$ teaspoon ground cayenne pepper

1 tablespoon grill seasoning, such as McCormick's Montreal Steak Seasoning

Zest of 1 lemon

2 tablespoons extra-virgin olive oil (EVOO), plus some for drizzling

2 pounds flank steak

1 bunch scallions

16 raw medium shrimp, deveined

Salt and freshly ground black pepper

1 teaspoon hot red pepper flakes

2 romaine lettuce hearts, chopped

4 ounces baby spinach leaves

$\frac{1}{4}$ cup fresh flat-leaf parsley (a couple of handfuls), chopped

$\frac{1}{2}$ red onion, chopped

DRESSING

    Juice of 1 lemon
2 tablespoons tomato paste
2 teaspoons Worcestershire sauce
3 tablespoons extra-virgin olive oil (EVOO) (eyeball it)
    Salt and freshly ground black pepper

Preheat a tabletop grill, grill pan, or outdoor grill to high.

Combine the first 10 ingredients in a shallow dish. Coat the flank steak in mixture and set aside for 10 to 15 minutes.

Trim the ends and an inch of the tops off of the scallions. Remove the tails from the deveined shrimp. Drizzle EVOO over both the scallions and the shrimp and season with salt, pepper, and hot red pepper flakes. Grill the scallions and shrimp for 2 minutes on each side. Then remove and reserve.

Place the meat on a grill pan and cook for 3 to 4 minutes on each side. Remove the meat to a plate, tent with foil, and let the juices settle for 5 minutes.

Combine the greens, parsley, and onion on a large platter or individual plates. Cut the grilled scallions into 1-inch pieces, scatter over the greens, then evenly distribute the grilled shrimp over the greens. In a small bowl mix the lemon juice, tomato paste, and Worcestershire and whisk in the EVOO. Season the dressing with salt and pepper and drizzle it back and forth over the arranged greens and scallions and shrimp. Slice the steak very thin against the grain on an angle with a sharp knife and arrange it over the salad.

Cobb Salad: Double the Meat and Hold the Lettuce!

A Cobb salad is usually a big mound of lettuce topped with strips of chopped chicken, bacon, avocado, tomatoes, hard-boiled egg, and blue cheese. I love it, but I've noticed that once I mix it up and start eating, my fork is busy fishing around the lettuce trying to catch all the chicken and bacon. So, I decided to hold the lettuce. I did, however, add some watercress, but that's for its great peppery flavor!

4 SERVINGS

- 3 garlic cloves, finely chopped
- 2 tablespoons grill seasoning, such as McCormick's Montreal Steak Seasoning
- 1 tablespoon hot sauce, such as Tabasco (eyeball it)
- 2 tablespoons Worcestershire sauce (eyeball it)
- 3 tablespoons red wine vinegar
- 1/3 cup extra-virgin olive oil (EVOO), plus some for drizzling
- 2 pounds flank steak
- 4 thin chicken breast cutlets
- 1 ripe Hass avocado
- 2 vine-ripe tomatoes, cut into wedges
- 1 bunch watercress, trimmed and roughly chopped
- 5 strips Ready Crisp parcooked bacon, crisped in microwave and chopped
  Juice of 1 lemon
  Salt and freshly ground black pepper
- 1/3 pound blue cheese (such as Maytag Blue), crumbled

Heat a grill pan or outdoor grill to high heat.

In a bowl mix the garlic, grill seasoning, hot sauce, Worcestershire sauce, and vinegar. Whisk in the EVOO. Divide the mixture between two shallow dishes. Add the flank steak to one and the thin chicken cutlets to the other. Toss to coat all of the meats thoroughly and marinate for 5 minutes.

While the flank steak and chicken are marinating, cut the avocado in half lengthwise, cutting around the pit. Separate the halves, then, using a spoon, scoop out the pit and scoop the avocado from its skin. Chop the avocado flesh into bite-size pieces and add to a mixing bowl. Add the tomatoes, watercress, and crisp chopped bacon. Dress the salad with the lemon juice, a generous drizzle of EVOO, and salt and pepper to taste.

Grill the flank steak for 6 to 7 minutes on each side. Grill the chicken cutlets for 3 to 4 minutes on each side. Remove both meats from the grill to a cutting board to rest for about 5 minutes. Thinly slice the flank steak on an angle, cutting the meat against the grain. Cut the chicken into thin strips. Add both meats to a platter or dinner plates. Top the meats with a mound of the salad and garnish with a generous dose of blue cheese crumbles. Eat and enjoy the lack of lettuce getting in your way!

Shish Kabob Salad

- 2 pounds boneless leg of lamb, cubed
- Juice and zest of 1 lemon
- Juice and zest of 1 orange
- 2 tablespoons grill seasoning, such as McCormick's Montreal Steak Seasoning
- 4 garlic cloves, finely chopped
- 1 teaspoon hot red pepper flakes
- 1 tablespoon ground cumin (a palmful)
- 2 teaspoons sweet paprika (²/₃ palmful)
- ½ teaspoon ground allspice
- A handful of fresh cilantro leaves, finely chopped
- 3 tablespoons extra-virgin olive oil (EVOO) (eyeball it)
- 1 cup plain yogurt
- A few drops of hot sauce, such as Tabasco
- 2 teaspoons ground coriander
- Salt and freshly ground black pepper
- ½ English (seedless) cucumber, cut in bite-size pieces
- 2 vine-ripe tomatoes, seeded and chopped
- 1 green bell pepper, cored, seeded, and diced into bite-size pieces
- ½ red onion, chopped
- 2 tablespoons chopped fresh dill or cilantro, for garnish

Preheat an outdoor grill or a grill pan to medium-high heat.

Thread the meat cubes onto metal skewers. In a shallow dish that will hold the skewers, combine the lemon zest and juice, orange zest and juice, grill seasoning, garlic, red pepper flakes, cumin, paprika, allspice, cilantro, and EVOO. Slather the marinade all over the kabobs. Let the kabobs hang out for 10 minutes, then grill for 8 to 10 minutes for medium rare, 12 to 15 minutes for medium well. Give them a quarter turn every couple of minutes as they cook.

While the meat is on the grill, prepare the salad. In a medium bowl, combine the yogurt, hot sauce, coriander, and salt and pepper to taste. Add the veggies to the bowl and toss to coat them in the spiced yogurt. Taste to adjust the seasonings.

Slide the meat off the skewers and serve the hot spiced lamb alongside the cool, chunky vegetable salad. Garnish the salad with your choice of chopped dill or some more cilantro.

Bresaola Salad

High in protein, with practically no carbs—this salad rocks and makes a great lunch or dinner!

4 SERVINGS

8 cups arugula
Juice of 1 lemon
Extra-virgin olive oil (EVOO), for drizzling
Coarse salt
6-ounce chunk of Parmigiano-Reggiano
1 pound bresaola (cured beef, like prosciutto; available at deli counter)
1 can (15 ounces) artichoke hearts in water, drained
4 sprigs fresh rosemary
A handful of fresh flat-leaf parsley
1/2 cup capers, drained
Aged balsamic vinegar, for drizzling (look for 6-plus years of age, widely available in many markets)

Place the arugula in a bowl and dress with lemon juice, EVOO, and salt. Divide the arugula among 4 dinner plates or place on a serving platter and mound the greens. Use a vegetable peeler to shred some cheese on top of the arugula. Arrange the bresaola in a thin layer all around the plate, draping it over the arugula. The plates or platter should look like a mound of beef. Thinly slice the artichokes, finely chop the rosemary and parsley, and slice the capers. Decoratively arrange the artichokes, chopped herbs, and capers all over the meat. Drizzle the completed salad with aged balsamic vinegar and serve.

Chicken Greek-a-Tikka Salad with Parsley-Feta Pesto

4 SERVINGS

- 1 cup plain yogurt
- 1 teaspoon ground coriander
- 1 teaspoon ground cumin
- 1 teaspoon dried oregano
- 1 tablespoon grill seasoning, such as McCormick's Montreal Steak Seasoning
- 2 to 2 1/2 pounds white-meat chicken, cut into bite-size cubes
- 1 romaine lettuce heart, chopped or torn
- 2 vine-ripe tomatoes, chopped
- 1/2 English (seedless) cucumber (the one wrapped in plastic), chopped
- 1/2 red onion, chopped
- 3 celery ribs, chopped
- 1/2 cup pitted kalamata olives
- 6 peperoncini hot peppers, chopped
  Juice of 1 lemon
  Extra-virgin olive oil (EVOO), for drizzling
  Salt and freshly ground black pepper

PARSLEY-FETA PESTO

- 1 cup fresh flat-leaf parsley
- 1/2 cup crumbled feta
- 1 garlic clove
- 1 teaspoon coarse black pepper
- 3 tablespoons chopped walnuts
- 1/4 cup extra-virgin olive oil (EVOO) (eyeball it)

Preheat a grill pan to high heat. Heat a toaster oven or oven to 250°F.

In a bowl, combine the yogurt, coriander, cumin, oregano, and the grill seasoning. Coat the chicken in the mixture, then thread the meat onto metal skewers. Brush the grill pan with oil and grill the meat for 5 to 6 minutes on each side.

Combine the chopped veggies, olives, and hot peppers on a large platter or in a serving bowl. Dress the salad very lightly in lemon juice, EVOO, and salt and pepper.

Place all ingredients for the pesto in the food processor except the EVOO. Turn the processor on and stream in EVOO until all is incorporated.

Place the grilled meat on the salad and top liberally with the pesto, streaming it back and forth over the salad and the meat.

Greek Village Vegetable Stacks

4 SERVINGS

	1-pound brick of Greek feta cheese, drained
1	large green bell pepper
1	English (seedless) cucumber (the one wrapped in plastic)
1	medium red onion
2	beefsteak tomatoes
	Coarse salt
2	or 3 sprigs fresh oregano
	A handful of fresh flat-leaf parsley
1	lemon
	Coarse black pepper
½	cup extra-virgin olive oil (EVOO)
1	cup kalamata olives

Carefully slice the brick of feta into 12 slices, ¼ to ½ inch thick each. Use a cheese wire or some dental floss to cut the cheese if it crumbles too easily when using a knife. Next, trim off both ends of the bell pepper and pull out the seeds and membranes. Thinly slice the pepper into 12 pieces, ¼ to ½ inch thick. Slice the cucumber even thinner, into ⅛-inch-thick rounds. Trim the ends off the onion as you did the pepper. Cut the outer layer of skin off, then trim one side with a shallow cut so that the whole onion sits

continued ....➤

stable on its side. Thinly slice the onion as you did the pepper, into 12 pieces. Slice the tomatoes in the same fashion as the onion, trimming off one side to stabilize it before slicing it across. Cut the tomatoes a little thicker, 6 slices per tomato. Season the tomatoes with a little coarse salt.

Strip the oregano leaves off the stems by holding stems at the top and gently pulling backward. Pile up the leaves on your cutting board and combine with the parsley leaves. Finely chop both, milling them together. To the chopped herbs, add the zest of the lemon. Trim the ends of the lemon and wedge it; reserve wedges. To the herb and lemon zest combination, add lots of fresh coarse black pepper—at least a full teaspoon and up to 2. Mix it in with your fingertips.

Arrange the cheese slices in a single layer on your work surface and scatter the herb mixture over the cheese slices.

Pour a puddle of EVOO on each plate or on a serving platter. Assemble stacks of Greek salad like this: sliced tomato, sliced onion, a layer of thin slices of cucumber, a slice of bell pepper, a slice of herb-crusted feta. Repeat twice. Each stack will have 3 layers, making a tower of Greek salad for each portion. Garnish each plate or the serving platter with olives and wedges of lemon.

Turkey Club Salad with Avocado Dressing

4 SERVINGS

- 12 slices Ready Crisp bacon or other microwave-ready sliced bacon
- 3 romaine lettuce hearts
- 2 cups pea shoots, radish spouts, or bean spouts
- 3 plum tomatoes, sliced
- 1/2 medium red onion, chopped
  Salt and freshly ground black pepper
- 1 1/2 pounds rotisserie turkey breast or thick-sliced deli roast turkey breast
- 2 ripe Hass avocados
  Zest and juice of 1 lemon
- 1 garlic clove
- 1 teaspoon salt
- 2 tablespoons red wine vinegar
- 1/3 cup extra-virgin olive oil (EVOO)
- 2 teaspoons Tabasco sauce (eyeball it)

Crisp the bacon in the microwave according to package directions. Remove it from the microwave and chop it. Of course, any bacon or turkey bacon that you have on hand may be substituted. These prerendered bacon products simply allow you to keep more heat out of the kitchen by giving you the option of a low-maintenance microwave preparation.

Chop the romaine lettuce and arrange on a large platter. Arrange a bed of pea shoots or sprouts on top of the lettuce, then arrange the tomatoes and red onion on top of that. Season the salad vegetables with salt and pepper, to your taste. Scatter the chopped bacon onto the salad.

Remove the rotisserie turkey from the bone with a sharp carving knife. Slice the rotisserie breast meat on an angle into strips. For thick-cut turkey from the deli, julienne the meat into 1/2-inch

continued ....➤

strips. Arrange the sliced turkey down the center of the salad platter.

Cut all around the ripe avocados down to the pit. Twist and separate the halved fruit. Remove the pit with a spoon, then scoop the flesh with a spoon into the bowl of a food processor. Add the lemon zest and juice to the food processor. Chop the garlic on a cutting board and mash with 1 teaspoon salt to make a paste. Add the garlic paste to the food processor. Add the red wine vinegar. Place a lid on the food processor and turn it on. While the blade is spinning, stream in EVOO and add hot sauce. Stop the processor, taste the dressing, and adjust the seasonings. Pour the dressing back and forth over the platter evenly when you are ready to serve this simple and so-cool salad meal.

Pancetta-Wrapped Chicken on Arugula-Fennel Salad with Orange Vinaigrette

4 SERVINGS

   1 cup (about 20 leaves) fresh basil

   2 handfuls fresh flat-leaf parsley

   1 garlic clove, smashed and peeled

     Zest and juice of 1 navel orange

     Salt and freshly ground black pepper

½ cup plus 2 tablespoons extra-virgin olive oil (EVOO)

   4 boneless, skinless chicken breasts (6 ounces each)

   4 thin slices pancetta (cured Italian bacon; available at deli counter)

   1 tablespoon Dijon mustard

   1 tablespoon red wine vinegar

   1 bulb fennel, trimmed, cored, and thinly sliced

   1 pound arugula (2 bunches), washed and trimmed of stems

Preheat the oven to 375°F.

In a food processor combine the basil, parsley, garlic, orange zest, and salt and pepper. With the processor running, stream in about ¼ cup of the EVOO. Process until it looks like a paste. Pour the herb mixture into a shallow dish. Add the chicken breasts and toss to coat the chicken completely. Unwind a slice of the pancetta and wrap it around the center of an herb-coated chicken breast. Repeat with the remaining chicken breasts.

Heat a large, heavy-bottomed skillet with a heat-safe handle with 2 tablespoons of the remaining EVOO (twice around the pan) over medium-high heat. Once you see the oil ripple, add the wrapped chicken breasts and brown for 2 minutes. Flip the chicken breasts and continue to brown for about 1 more minute. Transfer the skillet to the preheated oven and roast for about 10 minutes, or until the chicken is cooked through.

While the chicken is cooking, prepare the salad. Add the juice of the orange, Dijon mustard, and red wine vinegar to a small bowl. Whisk in the remaining ¼ cup of EVOO (eyeball it). In a salad bowl combine the thinly sliced fennel with the arugula. Add the dressing and toss to coat. Season the salad with salt and pepper to taste.

Slice the chicken wrapped in pancetta on an angle. Arrange the sliced chicken on top of a pile of the salad and serve.

TIDBIT

If you do not have a processor, use your blender for this herb sauce. If you don't do kitchen machines, you can finely chop all the herbs and garlic together until you run out of patience for the task. Transfer the garlic-herb paste to a bowl and mix in a little EVOO.

Chipotle-Glazed Chicken Breast and Grilled Chopped Veggie Salad

Chipotle in adobo sauce can be found in both small and large cans. They are smoked dried jalapeño peppers that are packed with flavor! In the can, they are soft and packed in vinegar and spices. If heat is not your thing, then use half of one chipotle pepper. The remainder of the chipotles can be frozen in a resealable plastic bag for other uses such as adding a smoky, spicy flavor to soups and stews or shaking up and waking up your everyday guacamole.

4 SERVINGS

- 5 tablespoons vegetable oil, plus some for drizzling
- ½ small yellow onion, chopped
- 3 garlic cloves, chopped
- 2 tablespoons tomato paste
- 2 tablespoons honey
- 2 chipotle peppers in adobo sauce, finely chopped
- ¼ cup plus 3 tablespoons cider vinegar
- 1 cup chicken stock or broth
- 1 medium zucchini, sliced lengthwise into ½-inch slices
- 1 medium yellow squash, sliced lengthwise into ½-inch slices
- 1 red bell pepper, cut in half, cored, and seeded
- 1 Granny Smith apple, cored and sliced into ½-inch rings
- 4 boneless, skinless chicken breasts (6 ounces each)
  Salt and freshly ground black pepper
- 1 16-ounce sack of coleslaw mix (on the produce aisle)
- 2 rounded tablespoons honey mustard, such as Gulden's Spicy Honey Mustard
- 1½ teaspoons ground cumin (half a palmful)
- 2 rounded tablespoons sour cream or plain yogurt

Preheat a grill pan or charcoal grill to high.

To make the chipotle glaze, in a small saucepot heat about 2 tablespoons of the vegetable oil over medium-high heat. Add the onion and garlic; cook for about 2 minutes, stirring frequently. Add the tomato paste, honey, chipotles, and ¼ cup cider vinegar, and cook for 1 minute. Add the chicken stock and cook for 10 minutes, or until the glaze has thickened. Reserve the sauce on low heat.

While the chipotle glaze is cooking, season the sliced veggies, apple, and the chicken breasts with salt and pepper. Drizzle with a generous amount of vegetable oil. Place the veggies, apple, and chicken on the grill. The veggies should be cooked for 3 to 4 minutes per side, or until they are well marked by the grill, then remove to cool slightly. The chicken should be cooked for 6 minutes per side. For the last 2 minutes of cooking time, baste the chicken using a pastry brush with the thickened chipotle glaze. Both sides of the chicken should be well coated with the glaze. Remove the chicken from the grill to rest while you put the rest of the grilled chopped veggie salad together.

Chop the cooled veggies into bite-size pieces and transfer to a salad bowl. Add the coleslaw mix. In a small bowl whisk together the honey mustard, cumin, and the remaining 3 tablespoons of cider vinegar; stream in the remaining 3 tablespoons of vegetable oil while you continue to whisk the dressing. Stir in the sour cream or yogurt. Season the dressing with salt and pepper. Pour the dressing over the veggies and toss to coat.

Slice the chicken breasts on an angle and serve them on top of a mound of the salad.

Warm Grilled Chicken Salad with Ginger-Soy Vinaigrette

4 SERVINGS

    3-inch piece fresh gingerroot, peeled
¼ cup tamari (dark aged soy sauce)
6 tablespoons vegetable oil
    Salt and freshly ground black pepper
4 portobello mushrooms, cleaned, stems discarded
6 thin chicken breast cutlets
2 tablespoons ground coriander
    Juice of 2 limes
1 tablespoon Dijon mustard
2 1-pound sacks of washed spinach, thick stems removed
3 tablespoons toasted sesame seeds (on the Asian foods aisle)

Preheat a charcoal grill or grill pan to high.

Grate or mince the ginger, add half to a shallow dish for the mushrooms, and reserve the other half in a bowl for the vinaigrette. To the shallow dish, add about 2 tablespoons of the tamari and about 3 tablespoons of the vegetable oil. Season with salt and pepper. Flip the portobello mushroom caps around in the marinade in the shallow dish. Place the mushroom caps on the grill and cook on each side for 4 to 5 minutes, until tender and cooked through.

Season the chicken cutlets with salt, pepper, and the ground coriander. Place the seasoned chicken cutlets on the grill and cook for 4 minutes per side, or until the chicken is cooked through.

Add the lime juice, Dijon mustard, and the remaining 2 tablespoons of tamari to the reserved ginger. Combine, then whisk in the remaining 3 tablespoons of vegetable oil.

Remove the mushrooms and chicken from the grill and slice into ½-inch slices. Toss the sliced chicken, sliced mushrooms, and the spinach with the dressing. Garnish with the toasted sesame seeds.

Grilled Chicken Caesar with Bacon-Herb-Parmesan "Croutons"

4 SERVINGS

- ½ cup extra-virgin olive oil (EVOO)
- 2 slices bacon, finely chopped
- 1½ cups grated Parmigiano-Reggiano
- 2 tablespoons fresh flat-leaf parsley (a handful), chopped
- 4 garlic cloves, chopped
- Juice of 2 lemons
- Salt and freshly ground black pepper
- 8 thin chicken breast cutlets (about 1¼ pounds)
- 2 tablespoons Dijon mustard
- 1 tablespoon Worcestershire sauce
- 3 romaine lettuce hearts, roughly chopped
- 3 hard-boiled eggs, chopped (you can get these in the salad bar area of the market, or make your own; see Tidbit, page 90)

Preheat the oven 400°F. Preheat a charcoal grill or grill pan to high.

Heat a small skillet over medium-high heat with 1 tablespoon of the EVOO (once around the pan). Add the chopped bacon and cook until really crispy, 2 to 3 minutes. Remove the bacon to a plate lined with a paper towel to drain and cool.

In a small bowl combine 1 cup of the grated cheese with the chopped parsley and cooled bacon. Mix to distribute the bacon and parsley evenly. Line a baking sheet with a piece of parchment paper. Pour the cheese mixture out onto the center of the baking sheet and with your fingers, spread out the cheese in an even and very thin layer. Give the pan a little shake to help you even it out. This way you will have a lacy web when the cheese melts. Place the baking sheet in the oven for 3 to 4 minutes, turning the pan midway through the cooking. If your oven has hot spots, you will

continued ....➤

have to turn it more often than just once to ensure even browning. Once the cheese has melted and is nice and golden brown, remove it from the oven to cool completely.

While the cheese is baking, prepare the chicken and the Caesar dressing. (But a little heads up: Don't forget about the Parmesan "croutons" because they go from golden brown to black in a blink of your eye.) Like I was saying, for the chicken, in a shallow dish combine half of the chopped garlic, half of the lemon juice, salt, pepper, and a generous drizzle of the EVOO. Add the chicken cutlets and toss to completely coat. Place the chicken on the hot grill and cook on each side for 3 to 4 minutes. Remove from the grill.

While the chicken is cooking, in a mixing bowl combine the remaining chopped garlic, the Dijon mustard, the Worcestershire sauce, the remaining lemon juice, and lots of freshly ground pepper. Whisk in about $\frac{1}{3}$ cup of the EVOO. Add the remaining $\frac{1}{2}$ cup of Parmigiano and stir to combine. In a salad bowl combine the romaine lettuce and the hard-boiled eggs. Dress with the Caesar dressing.

To serve, slice the cooled chicken into thin strips and divide among 4 plates. Top the chicken with the dressed romaine and hard-boiled egg. Gingerly remove the baked Parmesan from the pan, pulling on one of the corners of the parchment paper to help you lift it up and out. With your hands, crack the baked cheese into "croutons" or asymmetrical 1- to 2-inch pieces. Garnish the salad with the "croutons" and serve.

TIDBIT

Place eggs in a small saucepot and add enough water to cover them. Place over high heat. Once the eggs are at a simmer, turn the heat off, cover the pot, and let the eggs sit for 10 minutes. Drain off the hot water then shake the pan aggressively to crack the eggshells. Run the eggs under cold water, then peel.

Grilled Balsamic Chicken with Puttanesca Salad

4 SERVINGS

¼ cup capers, rinsed and dried
  Extra-virgin olive oil (EVOO), for drizzling, plus ¼ cup for dressing
1½ pounds thin chicken breast cutlets
2 tablespoons balsamic vinegar
  Coarse salt and coarse black pepper
3 romaine lettuce hearts, trimmed and chopped
½ cup fresh flat-leaf parsley (3 handfuls), chopped
½ cup pitted black olives, chopped
½ cup soft sun-dried tomatoes (in tubs or pouches in produce aisle), rough cut
2 garlic cloves, minced
3 tablespoons anchovy paste
2 tablespoons red wine vinegar

Preheat a toaster oven or conventional oven to 375°F. Spread the capers on a small baking sheet and drizzle EVOO over them. Place the capers in the oven and turn it off. Do not open the door. The capers will roast as the oven cools back down.

Preheat a grill pan, large nonstick skillet, tabletop grill, or outdoor grill to medium high.

Place the chicken on a platter and coat with the balsamic vinegar. Season the chicken with salt and pepper and drizzle with EVOO. Grill for 5 minutes on each side until cooked through.

In a large bowl combine the lettuce, parsley, olives, and sun-dried tomatoes. In a small bowl whisk the garlic and anchovy paste with the vinegar into a thick paste and then stream in EVOO to make the dressing. Toss the salad with dressing and season with black pepper to taste.

Chop or slice the chicken and arrange it on a platter. Top with piles of puttanesca salad. Garnish with the roasted capers.

Swordfish Bites with Puttanesca Salad

4 SERVINGS

- ½ cup capers, rinsed and dried
  Extra-virgin olive oil (EVOO), for drizzling, plus ¼ cup for dressing
- 2 pounds swordfish steak, trimmed of skin and dark connective tissue, then diced into bite-size cubes
  Zest of 2 lemons
- 4 garlic cloves, minced
- ½ cup fresh flat-leaf parsley (3 handfuls)
  Coarse salt and coarse black pepper
- 3 romaine lettuce hearts, trimmed and chopped
- ½ cup pitted black olives, chopped
- ½ cup soft sun-dried tomatoes (available in tubs or pouches in the produce section), rough cut
- 3 tablespoons anchovy paste
- 2 tablespoons red wine vinegar

Preheat a toaster oven or conventional oven to 375°F. Spread the capers onto a small baking sheet and drizzle EVOO over them. Place the capers in the oven and turn it off. Do not open the door. The capers will roast as the oven cools back down.

Preheat a large nonstick skillet to medium high.

Place the swordfish cubes on a platter. Make a pile on your cutting board of the lemon zest, half of the garlic, a handful of the parsley leaves, and some coarse salt and pepper. Chop and mash together the ingredients. Drizzle EVOO over the fish to coat it evenly and add the mash of garlic and lemon and parsley. Use your hands to evenly coat the fish. Add the fish to the hot pan and cook for 5 minutes, or until the cubes are opaque and firm.

Coarsely chop the remaining 2 handfuls of parsley and in a salad bowl combine with the lettuce, olives, and sun-dried tomatoes. In a small bowl whisk the remaining garlic and the anchovy paste with the vinegar into a thick paste and then stream in EVOO to make your dressing. Toss the salad with dressing and season with black pepper to taste.

Arrange the puttanesca salad on plates or on a platter. Remove the capers from the oven. Top the salad with the swordfish and the roasted capers and serve.

TIDBIT

Roasting gives capers a new flavor aspect. They become a little nutty and earthier and they pop when you bite down on them.

Tuna Skewers with Orange and Rosemary on Bitter Greens Slaw

4 SERVINGS

- 2 pounds tuna steak, cubed
- 2 tablespoons balsamic vinegar
- 3 to 4 tablespoons fresh rosemary, finely chopped
- Zest and juice of 1 large navel orange
- 1 tablespoon grill seasoning, such as McCormick's Montreal Steak Seasoning
- Extra-virgin olive oil (EVOO) for drizzling, plus 2 tablespoons for dressing
- 2 heads radicchio, shredded
- 2 heads Belgian endive, shredded
- 1/2 red onion, very thinly sliced
- 1 red bell pepper, halved, cored, seeded, and very thinly sliced
- 2 tablespoons red wine vinegar
- Salt and freshly ground black pepper

Preheat an outdoor grill, grill pan, or tabletop grill to high. Pile the cubed tuna onto metal skewers. Place them on a baking sheet or large shallow dish. Rub the balsamic vinegar into the fish. Combine the rosemary with the orange zest and grill seasoning. Drizzle EVOO over the skewers, then liberally coat the kabobs with the spice and herb mix. Cook the skewers a minute or so on each side, making quarter turns, for medium-rare fish; cook 2 minutes on each quarter turn for opaque, well-cooked fish.

While the fish cooks, mix the slaw by combining the shredded radicchio and endive with the onion and bell pepper. Juice the orange over the salad, then add the vinegar, followed by 2 tablespoons EVOO. Toss and season the slaw with salt and pepper.

Remove the fish from the skewers and serve on top of the bitter greens slaw.

Swordfish Kabobs on Fennel Slaw Salad

4 SERVINGS

2¼ to 2½ pounds swordfish steaks
½ cup fresh flat-leaf parsley (3 handfuls)
2 teaspoons coarse salt
3 garlic cloves
Zest of 2 lemons
1 teaspoon crushed hot red pepper flakes
Extra-virgin olive oil (EVOO), for drizzling, plus 3 tablespoons for salad
1 large bulb fennel with fronds
2 large heads radicchio, shredded
½ cup fresh flat-leaf parsley (3 handfuls), coarsely chopped
1 navel orange
2 tablespoons red wine vinegar
Salt and freshly ground black pepper

Preheat a grill pan, tabletop grill, or outdoor grill to high.

Trim the skin and dark connective tissue from the swordfish and cube. Pack the cubed meat onto metal skewers and place them on a baking sheet. Chop the parsley and set aside on your board. Pile up the coarse salt on the board. Pop the garlic from the skins and coarsely chop the garlic. Mix the garlic into the salt. Mash the garlic with the flat of your knife, using the salt like sandpaper to grind up the garlic into a paste. Mix the lemon zest into the garlic paste with your knife. Mix in the crushed pepper the same way. Gather half of the parsley with the back of your knife and combine it with the garlic-lemon-salt paste. Drizzle EVOO on the cubed fish and slather the kabobs with the herb and garlic paste. Cook the skewers for 7 to 8 minutes, 2 minutes on each side, a quarter turn at a time.

continued ....➤

While the fish cooks, assemble the slaw. Trim and chop a few tablespoons of the fennel fronds, then cut off the tough tops. Quarter the fennel bulb lengthwise and, using an angled cut into each quarter, remove the core. Thinly slice the fennel and place in a shallow platter with the fronds. Quarter the radicchio heads in the same manner and shred the lettuce. Add to the fennel and fronds. Mix in the remaining rough-cut parsley. Trim both ends of the orange and stand it end to end. Cut from top to bottom while turning the orange, cutting the skin off in strips. Cut the peeled orange in half and thinly slice each half-orange into half-moons. Mix the oranges with the salad. Dress the salad with about 2 tablespoons red wine vinegar and 3 tablespoons EVOO (eyeball it). Season the slaw salad with salt and pepper.

Remove the skewers from the heat. Cut one of the lemons you used for zest in half and squeeze the juice over the cooked fish. Juice the lemon cut side upright so the seeds remain in and with the lemon. Slide the fish free from the skewers and place it on top of the slaw salad.

Salmon Niçoise and Olive Dressing

If you are completely exhausted, substitute the salmon steaks with canned salmon. Buy one large can (18 ounces), drain, and arrange the chunks atop the salad. Buy hard-boiled eggs from the salad bar at the market, or boil your own (see Tidbit, page 90).

4 SERVINGS

Salt

1 pound trimmed green beans (many markets have packages of trimmed raw beans in the produce section)

6 tablespoons extra-virgin olive oil (EVOO)

4 6-ounce portions salmon fillets, skin off

Freshly ground black pepper

1/2 cup pitted kalamata olives or, if you are feeling industrious, get the tiny Niçoise black olives, but you will have to pit these yourself

4 anchovy fillets

1 garlic clove, smashed out of its skin

1 lemon, zested, then cut into wedges

2 tablespoons capers, drained

2 tablespoons sherry vinegar or red wine vinegar

6 cups mixed greens (1 sack)

1 small red or yellow bell pepper, cored, seeded, and cut into thin strips

1 handful fresh flat-leaf parsley, chopped

1 cup (about 20 leaves) fresh basil, torn

1/2 small red onion, thinly sliced

4 hard-boiled eggs

2 vine-ripe tomatoes, each cut into 8 wedges

Fill a large skillet with 1 inch of water, place it over high heat, and bring it to a boil. Add a large pinch of salt and the green beans. Cook the green beans for 1 to 2 minutes, drain, and run under cold water to stop the cooking process. Place the skillet

continued ....➤

back on the stove over medium-high heat with 2 tablespoons of EVOO (twice around the pan). Season the salmon steaks with salt and pepper. Add the salmon to the skillet and cook on both sides for 3 to 4 minutes or until cooked to desired doneness. While the salmon is cooking, make the olive dressing.

In a food processor or blender, combine the olives, anchovies, garlic, lemon zest, capers, and sherry or red wine vinegar. Process the dressing for about 30 seconds, then, while the machine is still running, add about 4 tablespoons of EVOO in a slow steady stream. Reserve the dressing.

On a platter toss together the cooled green beans, mixed greens, bell pepper, parsley, basil, and red onion. Cut the hard-boiled eggs into quarters. Arrange the eggs and tomato wedges around the platter. Arrange the cooked salmon steaks on top of the salad and drizzle with the olive dressing. Serve with lemon wedges for squeezing over the salmon.

Seafood Cobb Salad

4 SERVINGS

 3 garlic cloves, chopped
 1 teaspoon hot red pepper flakes
 ½ cup extra-virgin olive oil (EVOO), divided
   Zest and juice of 2 lemons
   Salt and freshly ground black pepper
 16 raw sea scallops
 16 raw jumbo peeled deveined shrimp
 1 ripe Hass avocado
 5 strips Ready Crisp parcooked bacon, crisped in microwave and chopped
 1 10-ounce sack of prewashed arugula
 2 bunches watercress, washed and trimmed
 1 pint grape tomatoes, some cut in half and some left whole
 1 cup (about 20 leaves) fresh basil, torn

20 blades of chives, coarsely chopped (about ½ cup)
 2 tablespoons dry mustard
 2 teaspoons Old Bay or other all-purpose seafood seasoning

On a shallow plate combine the garlic, red pepper flakes, about 3 tablespoons of the EVOO, half the lemon juice, and salt and pepper to taste. Coat the seafood in the mixture, keeping the shrimp and scallops in separate piles. Let the seafood hang out a few minutes.

While the seafood is marinating, cut the avocado in half lengthwise, cutting around the pit. Separate the halves and using a spoon, scoop out the pit, then scoop the avocado from its skin. Chop the avocado flesh into bite-size pieces and add to a salad bowl or large serving platter. Toss in with the bacon, arugula, watercress, tomatoes, basil, and chives.

For the dressing, in a small bowl combine the dry mustard, the Old Bay, the remaining lemon juice, the zest of both lemons, and salt and pepper. Whisk in about 3 tablespoons of EVOO (eyeball it). Pour the dressing over the salad and toss to combine and coat.

Preheat a large nonstick skillet over high heat with 1 tablespoon of EVOO (once around the pan). To the hot skillet, add the scallops and sear 3 to 4 minutes on each side or until caramel in color. Arrange them on the salad. Return the pan to the heat and add the shrimp. Sear and cook the shrimp 2 or 3 minutes, until pink and tails are curled toward heads. Transfer the shrimp to the salad and serve.

CHAPTER 5
THAT'S SOUPER!

*These super, souped-up soups and pots of chili
are hearty meals for lunch or dinner.*

Even if you cook for one or two, make a big pot because leftovers only
develop better flavor. Super Soups are even more "souper" the next day!

Indian Summer Turkey Chili

Choose any or all of the toppers for your chili.

4 SERVINGS

- 2 tablespoons extra-virgin olive oil (EVOO) (twice around the pan)
- 1¼ pounds ground turkey breast (99% lean) (average weight of 1 package)
- 3 tablespoons dark chili powder
- 1 tablespoon grill seasoning, such as McCormick's Montreal Steak Seasoning
- 1 tablespoon ground cumin (a palmful)
- 2 tablespoons Worcestershire sauce (eyeball it)
- 2 tablespoons hot sauce (eyeball it)
- 1 large yellow onion, quartered
- 2 bell peppers, any colors, cored, seeded, and cut in ¼-inch dice
- ¾ cup (½ bottle) beer (the alcohol cooks out)
- 1 can (28 ounces) tomato sauce or tomato purée
- ½ cup smoky barbecue sauce
- 1 cup frozen corn kernels

TOPPERS

Shredded cheeses: smoked white sharp Cheddar, such as Cabot brand; Pepper Jack, chipotle Cheddar, five-peppercorn Cheddar, Monterey Jack

Sliced canned jalapeños, drained

Salsas

Sour cream

Chopped green olives and pimientos

Chopped fresh cilantro

Heat a pot over medium to medium-high heat. Add the EVOO and the ground turkey. Season the meat with the chili powder, grill seasoning, cumin, Worcestershire, and hot sauce. Break up the meat with the back of a wooden spoon into small crumbles.

continued ....➤

Chop the onion, reserving one quarter of it for topping the chili. (Chop the reserved onion extrafine.) Brown the meat for 5 minutes, then add the onion and bell peppers and cook 10 minutes more. Add the beer and deglaze the pan, scraping up the drippings and cooking off the alcohol. Add the tomato sauce or purée, barbecue sauce, and corn and bring the chili to a bubble. Let the chili simmer for 10 minutes. Adjust the seasonings and heat level to your taste. Remove from the heat and serve with chopped raw onion and your choice of toppers.

TIDBIT

To make a double batch, heat two pots and make one batch in each pot, rather than using one massive pot that is hard to control.

Fire-Roasted Tomato, Beef, and Chipotle Chili

4 SERVINGS

- 4 slices applewood-smoked bacon or black pepper bacon
- 1 tablespoon vegetable oil (once around the pan)
- 2 pounds ground sirloin
- 2 tablespoons grill seasoning, such as McCormick's Montreal Steak Seasoning
- 4 garlic cloves, chopped
- 1 medium to large yellow onion, finely chopped
- 1 red bell pepper, cored, seeded, and chopped in ¼-inch dice
- 3 tablespoons ground chipotle chili powder (on spice aisle next to dark chili powder) or ½ small can chipotle chilies in adobo, chopped
- 6 ounces of beer
- 1 large can (28 ounces) fire-roasted tomatoes, such as Muir Glen brand
- 1 8-ounce brick of smoked white Cheddar or chipotle Cheddar, such as Cabot brand, shredded

Heat a medium pot over medium-high heat. Chop the bacon into 1-inch pieces. Add vegetable oil to the hot pot with the bacon. Brown the bacon until crisp and reserve on a plate lined with paper towels. To the bacon renderings and oil add the meat and break up with the back of a wooden spoon. Season the meat with grill seasoning. Let the meat brown for 3 minutes, then add the garlic, three-fourths of the onions, bell pepper, and the chipotle powder. The remaining raw chopped onions are for topping the chili.

Cook the meat and onions together for 5 or 6 minutes, then deglaze the pan with the beer. Add the tomatoes next and stir them in to combine. Simmer the chili over low heat for 10 minutes. Top bowls of chili with cheese, bacon, and finely chopped raw onion.

Green and White Lightning Chunky Chicken Chili

4 SERVINGS

- 2 tablespoons vegetable or canola oil (2 turns of the pan)
- 6 6-ounce boneless, skinless chicken breasts, cut into bite-size pieces
  Salt and freshly ground black pepper
- 1 medium yellow onion, thinly sliced
- 5 garlic cloves, finely chopped
- 1 jalapeño pepper, seeded and finely chopped
- 2 tablespoons ground cumin (2 palmfuls)
- 1 tablespoon ground coriander (a palmful)
- 1 cup mild or hot tomatillo salsa (green salsa on Mexican Foods aisle)
- 4 cups chicken stock or broth
- 1 can (15-ounces) cannellini or Great Northern beans
- 1 handful fresh cilantro, roughly chopped
- 1 handful fresh flat-leaf parsley, roughly chopped
  Juice of 1 lime
  Shredded Monterey Jack or Pepper Jack cheese, for garnish
- 1 individual lunch-box-size bag of corn chips, optional and not that dangerous

Heat a medium soup pot over medium-high heat with the vegetable oil. Add the chicken to the hot oil and season liberally with salt and pepper. Cook for 2 to 3 minutes, stirring frequently. Add the onion, garlic, jalapeño, cumin, and coriander and cook for 3 to 4 minutes, continuing to stir. Add the tomatillo salsa and the chicken stock. Bring the chili up to a simmer. Add half of the beans. With a fork thoroughly mash the other half of the beans, then add to the chili. This method will help to thicken the chili. Simmer the chili for 10 minutes. Remove the chili from the heat and add the cilantro, parsley, and lime juice.

Serve each bowl of chili with a little shredded Monterey Jack cheese on top. Oh, and go ahead, have a chip or two! I crush up a small bag and stir them right in!

CONFESSION

To be honest, I eat chili as an excuse to eat corn chips. I rarely need a spoon at all: one chip, two chips, three chips . . . well, it can get ugly is all I'm saying. To help keep my corn chip obsession in check and still feel satisfied, I buy one individual lunch-box-size bag of chips. This way I don't have that big gorgeous bag of chips dangerously calling my name from the cupboard. If I don't have them, I don't eat them. I exert my self-control at the supermarket.

STOUPS

These are extra hearty—thicker than a soup and not quite a stew.

Double-the-Sausage and Kale Stoup with Wrapped and Stuffed Green Jumbo Olive Snacks

4 SERVINGS

     2 tablespoons extra-virgin olive oil (EVOO) (twice around the pan)
    ¾ pound diced chorizo, casing removed
    ¾ pound diced andouille sausage
     1 large onion, chopped
     1 red bell pepper, cored, seeded, and chopped
     4 to 6 garlic cloves, chopped
     1 bay leaf, fresh or dried
     1 pound kale, coarsely chopped
       Salt and freshly ground black pepper
     1 can (15 ounces) chickpeas, drained and rinsed
     1 can (15 ounces) diced tomatoes
     1 quart chicken stock or broth
       Several drops of hot sauce, such as Tabasco, to taste
    ¼ pound manchego cheese in a chunk
    20 jumbo pitted green olives
    10 slices Serrano ham or prosciutto di Parma
    20 blades of fresh chives
       A handful of fresh flat-leaf parsley, chopped

Heat a deep pot over medium-high heat. Add the EVOO, chorizo, and andouille and sear the sausages for 1 to 2 minutes, then add the onion, bell pepper, garlic, and bay leaf. Cook for 5 minutes, stirring occasionally.

Add the kale to the pot. Cover the pot and wilt the greens, 2 minutes. Season the greens with salt and pepper. Add the chickpeas, tomatoes, and stock to the pot and bring the stoup to a full boil. Reduce the heat back to medium and cook 10 minutes longer. Add hot sauce to your taste.

While the stoup is cooking, start on your snack. Cut the manchego into small enough chunks that will fit into where the pit was in the jumbo green olive; you will need 20. Stuff each olive with the small chunk of cheese. Cut the slices of ham in half across. Bundle the ham around the olives and tie off with a chive blade. Pile up your bundles and start snacking!

Finish the stoup by removing the bay leaf and adding the chopped parsley.

TIDBIT

Chorizo is a garlicky, spicy pork sausage that is used frequently in both Spanish- and Mexican-style dishes. Andouille sausage is a smoked spicy sausage that you have probably had before if you have ever had Cajun-style cuisine. It is flavored with garlic, paprika, cayenne, and thyme. Both are located in the packaged-meats section of the market near kielbasa, franks, and wursts.

Cajun Jumble-laya Stoup

This jumble is a lot like jambalaya, so I call it a Jumble-laya.

This is one of those flexible recipes. You can substitute turkey or tender cuts of pork and beef for the chicken. Go all seafood by bumping up the amount of shrimp and adding crabmeat at the end to just heat it through.

Andouille sausage is a spicy, smoky sausage with a flavor that packs a punch. It is used in Cajun-style food and is a staple in gumbo and jambalaya. Is okra not your thing? Substitute frozen defrosted French-cut green beans

4 SERVINGS

- 2 tablespoons vegetable oil
- 1 pound andouille sausage, sliced on an angle into $1/2$-inch-thick slices (found in packaged meats near kielbasa)
- 2 pounds chicken tenders, cut into bite-size pieces
  Salt and freshly ground black pepper
- 1 medium yellow onion, sliced
- 3 large garlic cloves, chopped
- 3 celery ribs, chopped
- 1 green bell pepper, quartered, then sliced into thin strips
- 1 red bell pepper, quartered, then sliced into thin strips
- 4 sprigs fresh thyme
- 2 cups chicken stock or broth
- 1 cup tomato sauce or V-8 juice
- $1/4$ cup hot sauce, such as Frank's Red Hot (eyeball it)
- 1 pound raw medium shrimp, peeled and deveined
- 8 ounces ($1/2$ bag) whole or chopped frozen okra, defrosted
  A handful of fresh flat-leaf parsley, chopped
- 4 scallions, green and white parts, thinly sliced

Heat a large, deep skillet over high heat with the vegetable oil. Add the andouille sausage and brown for 2 to 3 minutes. Move the andouille sausage to one side of the pan and add the chicken tenders. Season the meat with salt and pepper. Continue to cook for another 3 minutes, until the chicken starts to brown. Stir to combine the chicken with the andouille sausage, then add the onion, garlic, celery, green and red bell peppers, and thyme sprigs. Cook, stirring frequently, for 5 minutes. Add the chicken stock, tomato sauce, and hot sauce and bring up to a boil. Add the shrimp and okra, cover the pot, and simmer for 5 minutes or until the shrimp are firm and pink. Uncover the stoup and stir. Turn the heat off, stir in the parsley and scallions, and serve.

Chorizo Chicken Stoup, Mixed Greens, and Sherry Vinaigrette

4 SERVINGS

  2 tablespoons extra-virgin olive oil (EVOO), plus some for drizzling
  1 pound chorizo sausage, casing split and removed
  2 pounds chicken tenders, cut into bite-size pieces
    Salt and freshly ground black pepper
½ tablespoon ground cumin (half a palmful)
  1 medium yellow onion, chopped
  3 garlic cloves, chopped
  1 yellow bell pepper, cored, seeded, and diced
  3 celery ribs, chopped
¼ cup good-quality aged sherry vinegar, divided
  2 cups chicken stock or broth
  1 can (28 ounces) diced tomatoes
  1 can (15 ounces) chickpeas, partially drained
  2 oranges
  6 cups (1 sack) mixed baby greens
¼ cup toasted sliced almonds (optional)
  3 tablespoons finely chopped fresh cilantro leaves

Heat a large soup pot over high heat with 2 tablespoons EVOO (twice around the pan). Once you see a ripple in the oil, add the sliced chorizo and cook, stirring frequently, for 2 minutes. Remove the chorizo with a slotted spoon and reserve. Add the

continued ....➤

chicken to the pot and season with salt, pepper, and cumin. Brown the chicken on all sides for 3 to 4 minutes. Add the reserved chorizo back to the pot along with the onion, garlic, bell pepper, and celery; cook for 3 minutes, stirring frequently. Add 1 tablespoon of the sherry vinegar and stir, then add the chicken stock, diced tomatoes, and chickpeas. Bring the stoup to a simmer, turn the heat down to medium low, and simmer for 10 minutes. While the stoup is cooking, prepare the salad.

Remove and reserve the zest of the two oranges. With a paring knife, cut the skin and white pith from both oranges, being sure to remove it all. Slice the oranges into disks. In a salad bowl combine the orange disks with the mixed greens. Dress the salad with the remaining sherry vinegar and a generous drizzle of EVOO. Season the salad with salt and pepper and toss to coat. Add the toasted almonds, if using.

To finish the stoup, remove it from the heat and stir in the reserved orange zest and chopped cilantro. Taste the stoup and adjust the seasonings.

Taco Stoup with a Taco Toppings Salad

4 SERVINGS

    4 tablespoons extra-virgin olive oil (EVOO), divided
1½ pounds ground sirloin
    1 tablespoon ground cumin
    1 tablespoon ground coriander
    1 tablespoon chili powder
 ½ tablespoon dried oregano
    1 large yellow onion, chopped
    3 garlic cloves, chopped

Salt and freshly ground black pepper

1 can (15 ounces) stewed tomatoes

1 quart chicken stock or broth

3 limes

1/3 cup mild taco sauce (eyeball it)

1 head iceberg lettuce, shredded

1/2 pint cherry or grape tomatoes, cut in half

1 handful fresh cilantro leaves, chopped

1 handful fresh flat-leaf parsley, chopped

1 cup good-quality sharp Cheddar cheese, shredded

Sour cream, for garnish

Heat a medium soup pot over medium-high heat with 2 table-spoons EVOO (twice around the pan). Add the ground sirloin. Brown the meat, breaking it up with a wooden spoon. Season it with the cumin, coriander, chili powder, oregano, onion, garlic, salt, and pepper. Stir to combine and continue to cook for 5 minutes. Add the stewed tomatoes and chicken stock, then bring the stoup up to a boil. Reduce the heat and simmer for 10 minutes. While the stoup is cooking, prepare the taco toppings salad.

In a small bowl combine the juice of 2 limes, the taco sauce, salt and pepper. Whisk in 2 tablespoons of EVOO. Reserve the dressing.

In a salad bowl combine the shredded lettuce, tomatoes, half of the chopped cilantro, the parsley, and grated Cheddar cheese. Pour the dressing over the salad and toss to combine.

Squeeze the juice of the remaining lime into the stoup. Ladle the stoup into serving bowls and garnish with a small dollop of sour cream and a sprinkle of cilantro.

Quick Cioppino

- 3 tablespoons extra-virgin olive oil (EVOO) (3 turns of the pan)
- 4 sprigs fresh thyme
- 4 garlic cloves, smashed
- 1 teaspoon crushed hot red pepper flakes
- 2 medium onions, quartered and thinly sliced
- 2 celery ribs with leafy tops from the heart, chopped
  Salt and freshly ground black pepper
- 2/3 cup white vermouth or 1 cup dry white wine
- 1 15-ounce can chunky-style crushed tomatoes
- 2 cups chicken stock or broth
- 2 pounds cod
  A wedge of fresh lemon
- 24 mussels, debearded and scrubbed
- 1/2 cup fresh flat-leaf parsley (a couple of handfuls), coarsely chopped

Heat a large, deep skillet over medium-high heat. Add the EVOO, thyme sprigs, garlic, and red pepper flakes and stir for 30 seconds, then add the onions and celery and season with salt and pepper. Cook for 5 minutes, then add the vermouth to deglaze the pan. Reduce the liquid by half, a minute or two. Add the tomatoes and stock and bring to a bubble. Dress the cod with a little lemon juice and salt and cut it into large chunks. Nestle the cod chunks into the bubbling pot so the liquids surround the fish. Cook the cod for 3 minutes, then add a layer of mussels to the pan and cover. Cook for 5 minutes longer, or until the mussels open. Discard any unopened mussels. Carefully stir the parsley in and remove the thyme stems. Ladle the stew into shallow bowls and serve.

Oktoberfest Stoup

4 SERVINGS

- 2 tablespoons vegetable oil
- 2 tablespoons butter, cut into pats
- 3 knockwursts, diced into 1-inch cubes
- 3 bratwursts, diced into 1-inch cubes
- 1 red onion, quartered and thinly sliced
- 2 pounds red cabbage, quartered and shredded
- 1 teaspoon caraway seeds
  Salt and freshly ground black pepper
- 1 12-ounce bottle dark beer
- 1 quart veal or chicken stock
- 2 cups tomato sauce
- 2 tablespoons Worcestershire sauce
- 1 bay leaf, fresh or dried
- 3 tablespoons finely chopped flat-leaf parsley
- 2 Red or Golden Delicious apples, peeled and diced
  Juice of $1/2$ lemon

Heat a big soup pot over medium-high heat. Add 1 tablespoon of the vegetable oil and half the butter. When the butter melts into the oil, add the cubed wursts and brown them on all sides, 5 minutes. Remove the browned sausages and add the remaining tablespoon each of oil and butter. When the butter melts into the oil, add the onion and cook for 2 minutes. Add the cabbage and caraway, season with salt and pepper, and stir. Cook the cabbage for 10 minutes, stirring frequently. Add the beer and cook down 1 minute. Add the stock, tomato sauce, Worcestershire, and bay leaf and stir to combine. Add the wursts back to the pot. Cover the pot and bring the stoup up to a boil, 2 or 3 minutes. Remove the lid and simmer for 5 to 10 minutes longer, until the cabbage is tender. Remove the bay leaf. Combine the parsley, apple, and lemon juice in a small bowl. Ladle the stoup into shallow bowls and top with generous spoonfuls of the flavored apples to stir into the stoup as you eat it.

Grilled Tomato Stoup with Prosciutto and Mozzarella Portobellos

4 SERVINGS

- 4 large portobello mushrooms, stems discarded
  Salt and freshly ground black pepper
- 2 tablespoons extra-virgin olive oil (EVOO), plus some to drizzle
- 1 medium yellow onion, chopped
- 4 garlic cloves, chopped
- 1 teaspoon crushed hot red pepper flakes
- 4 sprigs fresh thyme
- 1 quart chicken stock or broth
- 8 large plum tomatoes, cut in half lengthwise
- 1 slice crusty bread, optional
- 4 slices prosciutto or other good-quality ham
- 4 slices fresh mozzarella cheese
- 4 tablespoons store-bought pesto (optional)

Preheat the oven to 450°F.

Preheat an outdoor grill or indoor grill pan on high.

Place the portobello mushrooms on a baking sheet. Season both sides with salt and pepper and arrange the mushrooms gill side up. Drizzle the gill sides with a little EVOO. Put them in the oven and roast for 12 minutes, or until cooked through.

While the mushrooms are roasting, start the soup. Heat a soup pot over medium-high heat with 2 tablespoons of EVOO (twice around the pan). Add the onion, garlic, red pepper flakes, and thyme sprigs. Cook for 2 to 3 minutes, then add the chicken stock and bring up to a boil. Reduce heat to medium low and simmer the stoup for 10 minutes.

Drizzle EVOO over the plum tomatoes and season them with salt and pepper. Place on the grill and char on all sides, about 5 minutes. Drizzle the slice of bread with a little EVOO, place on the grill, and cook until well marked on both sides, 2 minutes. Remove the tomatoes and bread slice from the grill and roughly chop. Add them to a blender with about one fourth of the simmering broth. Purée for about 1 minute. Add the tomato-bread purée to the simmering soup and continue to cook for 5 minutes.

Once the mushrooms are cooked, top each one with a slice of prosciutto and a slice of mozzarella. Return the mushrooms to the oven to melt the cheese, about 2 minutes.

To serve, ladle into bowls and garnish with about a tablespoon of pesto. Serve the prosciutto- and cheese-topped mushrooms alongside.

CONFESSION

This soup is tasty without the bread slice, but I would never make it that way. I like the consistency better with a little bread. This soup is already a HUGE reduction in carbs from its predecessor, *papa al pomodoro*, bread and tomato soup from Florence, Italy. But it's up to you—it all depends on how many carbs you have had the day you make the soup and how uptight you are feeling about it. The soup really is great with or without the grilled bread. I confess, I cannot give it up entirely.

Meatball and Sausage Pizza Stoup

The meatball dumplings in the stoup taste okay without the 2 tablespoons of bread crumbs, but being a Sicilian girl, I simply cannot make a meatball with *no* bread crumbs. This is as close as I can force myself. It's only 2 tablespoons. Negligible carbs, but all the difference mentally and the consistency is really better for it.

4 SERVINGS

- 2 tablespoons extra-virgin olive oil (EVOO) (twice around the pan)
- 1 pound bulk Italian sausage, sweet or hot
- 4 garlic cloves, 2 crushed and 2 minced
- 1 large yellow onion, chopped
- 1 carrot, peeled and chopped
- 2 celery ribs, chopped
- 1 quart chicken stock or broth
- 1 can (15 ounces) pizza sauce
- 1 pound ground beef, pork, and veal mix or ground sirloin
- ½ cup grated Parmigiano-Reggiano (a couple of handfuls), plus more to pass at table
- 2 tablespoons Italian bread crumbs
- 1 egg yolk, beaten
  Salt and freshly ground black pepper
- ½ teaspoon allspice
  A handful of chopped fresh flat-leaf parsley

Heat a medium soup pot over medium-high heat. Add EVOO (twice around the pan) and the sausage. Break up the sausage with the back of a wooden spoon and brown it, about 3 minutes. Add the 2 crushed garlic cloves and the chopped onion, carrot, and celery. Stir to combine and cook for 5 minutes. Add the chicken stock and pizza sauce and raise heat to high to bring to a boil.

Meanwhile, in a bowl mix the ground meat with the minced garlic, grated cheese, bread crumbs, egg yolk, salt and pepper, and allspice. Form bite-size balls and drop them into boiling liquid. The meatballs will cook like dumplings in about 8 minutes. When all of the balls have been added and the stoup returns to a boil, reduce heat to simmer. Cook for 8 to 10 minutes. Add the parsley, stir, and ladle into shallow bowls. Top with a little grated cheese at table.

Red Snapper in Crazy Water (Acqua Pazza)

4 SERVINGS

2½ pounds red snapper fillet, cut into 3-inch chunks
    Salt and freshly ground black pepper
1½ tablespoons Old Bay or other seafood seasoning blend (a palmful and half again)
 3 tablespoons extra-virgin olive oil (EVOO) (three turns of the pan)
 1 teaspoon crushed hot red pepper flakes
 3 garlic cloves, crushed and peeled
 1 can flat anchovy fillets
 1 cup white wine
 ¼ cup (6 to 8 pieces) soft sun-dried tomatoes, not in oil (on the produce aisle), coarsely chopped
 3 tablespoons capers, drained
 4 scallions, chopped
 1 quart chicken stock or broth
    A handful of fresh flat-leaf parsley, chopped

Season the fish pieces with salt, pepper, and Old Bay. Heat a large, deep skillet over medium-high heat. Add the EVOO, hot red pepper flakes, garlic, and anchovies. Melt the anchovies into the oil. Add the snapper, skin side down, and crisp the skin. Turn and brown the fish for 3 to 4 minutes. Add the wine and deglaze the pan (lift up drippings), then add the sun-dried tomatoes, capers, and scallions and stir in the chicken stock. Stir the stoup gently so you do not break up the fish. Bring the broth to a simmer and cook for another 3 to 5 minutes to combine flavors.

Serve the fish in shallow bowls with plenty of crazy broth. Garnish with parsley.

Fish Chowder

- 1 tablespoon extra-virgin olive oil (EVOO) (once around the pan)
- 5 slices bacon, chopped
- 1 small yellow onion, chopped
- 2 celery ribs and their greens, finely chopped
- 4 sprigs fresh thyme
- 2 garlic cloves, chopped
  Salt and freshly ground black pepper
- 2 tablespoons flour
- 1 small baking potato, peeled and thinly sliced
- 1 quart chicken stock or broth
- 1 cup heavy cream or half-and-half
- 1 8-ounce bottle clam juice
- 2 pounds lean, flaky fish such as cod, haddock, halibut, monkfish, or tilapia, skinned and cut into 2- to 3-inch pieces
  Hot sauce, to taste
- 3 tablespoons fresh flat-leaf parsley, chopped (optional)

Heat a large soup pot over medium-high heat with the EVOO. Add the bacon and cook until crisp, about 3 minutes. Remove the crispy bacon to a plate lined with paper towels and reserve. Add the onion, celery, thyme sprigs, garlic, and salt and pepper to the pot and cook for about 3 minutes, mixing it every now and then. Add the flour to the vegetables, stirring to distribute, and cook for 1 minute. Add the thinly sliced potato, then whisk in the chicken stock, heavy cream, and clam juice. Bring the mixture up to a simmer and cook for 10 minutes. Add the fish and continue to gently simmer for 5 minutes. Turn the heat down a little if the pot is boiling rather than simmering. Add the desired amount of hot sauce and taste for seasoning; add more salt and pepper accordingly. To serve, carefully ladle the soup into bowls, trying not to break up the fish too much. Garnish each bowl with a little of the reserved crispy bacon and some chopped parsley. Serve the soup alongside a simple mixed green salad with your favorite salad dressing.

Thai Chicken Noodle Soup

4 SERVINGS

- 2 tablespoons vegetable oil (twice around the pan)
- 1 medium yellow onion, quartered and thinly sliced
- 3 garlic cloves, finely chopped
- 2 poblano or Anaheim peppers, seeded and thinly sliced

  Salt and freshly ground black pepper
- 1 cup shredded carrots (in pouches on the produce aisle)
- 6 cups (1½ quarts) chicken stock or broth
- 2 pounds chicken tenders, cut into bite-size chunks
- 1 small bundle from a 3.75-ounce package of bean thread noodles (there are usually 3 bundles in 1 package; recommended brand Kame)
- 3 tablespoons fresh cilantro leaves, chopped
- 15 fresh basil leaves, roughly chopped

  Juice of 1 lime

Heat a large, heavy-bottomed soup pot with the vegetable oil over high heat. Once you see the oil ripple, add the onion, garlic, and sliced peppers. Season the vegetables with salt and pepper and cook, stirring frequently, for 2 minutes. Add the carrots and 6 cups chicken stock. Cover with a lid and bring up to a simmer. Once simmering, add the chicken and noodles and simmer for 10 minutes more. Remove the soup from the heat and add the cilantro, basil, and the lime juice.

Noodle-Free Chicken Soup

This is a great late-night snack or easy lunch. It's my version of *stracciatelle* or "rag" soup. Basically, it's an Italian egg-drop soup. I make mine really full of egg "rags" or ribbons because when I eat chicken noodle soup I would make a bowl of noodles with a little broth. It's best to eat this really fresh and hot, so if you're cooking for one or two, just cut the recipe in half.

4 SERVINGS

    2 quarts chicken stock or broth
    8 eggs
  1/2 teaspoon grated nutmeg
    1 teaspoon freshly ground black pepper
  1/4 cup grated Parmigiano-Reggiano, plus some to pass at table
    3 tablespoons finely chopped fresh flat-leaf parsley

Bring the stock to a boil in a medium soup pot, then reduce heat to medium to have a good strong simmer going on. Beat the eggs with the nutmeg, pepper, and cheese. Add the eggs to the soup pot and stir them in with a whisk, swirling in a figure-eight pattern, making the eggs into rags in the soup. Ladle into shallow bowls and garnish with generous sprinkles of parsley and more cheese.

TIDBIT

Buy stock or broth in aseptic boxes rather than cans. They might cost a little more, but the stocks especially have great slow-cooked flavor that really makes fast-cooked food taste rich. Plus, whatever you don't use can go directly into the refrigerator, without having to transfer it from a can. If I know I am not going to use my remainder stock within the next few days, I will transfer it to a resealable plastic bag and freeze it flat. (I have had a small revolution of freezer storage space since embracing the freezing of things flat.)

Cream of Cheddar Soup and Lime Chicken Avocado Salad

2 tablespoons butter

1 large yellow onion, chopped

3 garlic cloves, chopped

1 teaspoon crushed hot red pepper flakes

Salt and freshly ground black pepper

2 tablespoons ground cumin

2 tablespoons flour

1 quart chicken stock or broth

1 cup heavy cream

5 tablespoons extra-virgin olive oil (EVOO)

5 thin chicken breast cutlets

1 tablespoon ground coriander

2 limes

1 ripe Hass avocado

½ head iceberg lettuce, shredded

½ pint cherry tomatoes, cut in half

¼ cup fresh cilantro leaves, chopped

4 cups good-quality aged Cheddar cheese, grated

Heat a soup pot over medium heat with the butter. When the butter melts, add the onion, garlic, red pepper flakes, salt, pepper, and 1 tablespoon of the cumin (a palmful). Cook for 3 minutes. Add the flour and cook for 1 minute more. Whisk in the chicken stock and heavy cream, bring up to a simmer, and cook for 10 minutes.

Preheat a large skillet over medium-high heat with 2 tablespoons of the EVOO (twice around the pan). Season the chicken breasts with the remaining tablespoon of cumin, the coriander, and salt and pepper; add to the hot skillet and cook for 2 to 3 minutes on each side, or until cooked through. Remove the chicken to the cutting board, squeeze the juice of 1 lime over the chicken, and allow it to cool slightly.

Cut the avocado in half lengthwise, cutting around the pit. Separate the halves and using a spoon, scoop out the pit and then scoop the avocado from its skin. Chop the avocado flesh into bite-size pieces. Add to a mixing bowl. To the avocado add the shredded iceberg lettuce, tomatoes, and cilantro. Cut the chicken into thin strips and add to the bowl. Squeeze the juice of the remaining lime over the salad and drizzle with the remaining 3 tablespoons of EVOO. Season with salt and pepper and toss to coat.

To finish the soup, turn the heat off. While whisking, add the grated Cheddar cheese in 3 additions. Serve the Cheddar soup immediately alongside the lime chicken avocado salad.

TIDBIT

Anything we make is only as good as the ingredients we put in it. The cheese is the big flavor in this soup, so look for good-quality Cheddar that has a super-sharp, deep Cheddar flavor.

CHAPTER 6

WELL-ROUNDED SQUARE MEALS

One problem with living a low-carb life is
that all your loved ones, family and even friends, who come over
for dinner are subjected to eating low-carb, too.
The menus in this section are hearty, rich in flavor, and tasty
enough to disguise the missing carbs, so carbers and
low-carbers alike can live, and eat, together in peace.

Sesame-Crusted Red Snapper with Ginger-Dressed Snappy Veggies

4 SERVINGS

2-inch piece fresh gingerroot, peeled and grated or minced
1 small jalapeño pepper, seeded and finely chopped
3 tablespoons rice wine vinegar or white wine vinegar (eyeball it)
Salt and freshly ground black pepper
5 tablespoons vegetable oil
10 radishes, thinly sliced
1 English (seedless) cucumber (the one wrapped in plastic), thinly sliced
1 yellow bell pepper, seeded, quartered, and cut into thin strips
4 8-ounce portions red snapper fillet, skin on
½ cup sesame seeds, untoasted (available on spice aisle)
1 bunch watercress, trimmed of thick stems
1 cup (about 20 leaves) fresh basil, coarsely chopped
¼ cup toasted unsalted peanuts, coarsely chopped

In a salad bowl combine the ginger, jalapeño, vinegar, salt, and pepper. In a slow steady stream, whisk in 3 tablespoons of the vegetable oil. Add the radishes, cucumber, and bell pepper and toss to coat. Let the veggies marinate at room temperature while you prepare the sesame-crusted snapper.

With a sharp paring knife, score the skin side of the snapper fillets: Slash 3 ⅛-inch-deep cuts across the width of the fish. Season both sides of the fish with salt and pepper. Sprinkle and then gently press the sesame seeds onto both sides of the fish. Heat a large nonstick skillet over medium-high heat with the remaining 2 tablespoons of vegetable oil (twice around the pan). When the pan is hot, add the seasoned fish to the skillet skin side down. Sauté the snapper for 4 minutes, and if you find that the fillets bubble up in the center section, carefully press each fillet down with a fish spatula. Flip the

continued ....➤

fillets and continue to cook on the second side for 3 minutes, or until the fish is cooked through and opaque. While the fish is cooking on the second side, finish off the ginger-dressed snappy veggies.

To the marinating vegetables add the watercress, basil, and peanuts. Toss to combine.

To serve, distribute the snappy veggies among four plates and top with the sesame-crusted snapper.

Swordfish and Chorizo Kabobs on Mostly-Vegetable Saffron Rice

4 SERVINGS

Juice of 2 lemons
4 garlic cloves, minced
¼ cup fresh cilantro (a handful)
½ cup fresh flat-leaf parsley (a couple of handfuls)
2 teaspoons crushed hot red pepper flakes
Coarse salt
¼ cup plus 1 tablespoon extra-virgin olive oil (EVOO)
2 pounds swordfish steak, trimmed of skin and dark connective tissue and cubed
¾ pound chorizo, casing removed and cut into 2-inch chunks
2 tablespoons butter
2 tablespoons fresh thyme leaves stripped from stems and chopped
1 small zucchini, diced
1 red bell pepper, cored, seeded, and diced
1 small yellow onion, diced
½ cup white enriched rice
1 small head cauliflower, cut into small florets
2 cups chicken stock or broth
Freshly ground black pepper
¼ teaspoon saffron threads (a healthy pinch)

Preheat an outdoor grill or indoor grill pan to medium high.

To a shallow dish add the lemon juice and garlic. Pile the cilantro and parsley together and finely chop them. Pile the green herbs into the dish. Add the red pepper flakes and a generous dose of coarse salt and the ¼ cup of EVOO. Mix the marinade and add the fish. Coat the fish evenly with the marinade, then thread it onto metal skewers. Thread the chorizo onto another skewer with cut sides facing out to expose them to the grill and so they will get good markings. Reserve the skewers.

Heat a deep, medium-size skillet over medium-high heat. Add the tablespoon of EVOO and the butter. When the butter melts into the oil, add the thyme, zucchini, bell pepper, onion, and rice. Stir and sauté the mixture for 3 minutes, then add the cauliflower and stock and season with salt and pepper. Stir in saffron threads and bring the liquid up to a bubble. Cover the pan tightly and reduce the heat to simmer. Cook for 17 minutes, or until the rice is tender.

Place the skewers on the grill when the mostly-vegetable rice has cooked for 5 minutes with the lid on. Cook the fish for 8 to 10 minutes, until opaque, turning every couple of minutes. Cook the chorizo for 2 to 3 minutes on each side to get good markings; the sausage is already fully cooked, you are just warming it and marking it.

Uncover the vegetables and rice and stir. Pile portions of the mostly-vegetables and saffron rice on plates. Remove the swordfish and chorizo from their skewers and combine them. Pile the fish and cooked chorizo on top of the veggie and rice mixture and serve.

RECIPISTORY

This is a hugely reduced-carb alternative to paella, a mostly rice, seafood, and sausage dish I used to entertain with often. Now, with no one eating carbs, paella would actually be rude to serve. This is my knockoff.

Citrus Crab Cakes with Sweet and Bitter Salad

4 SERVINGS

3 tablespoons extra-virgin olive oil (EVOO), plus some for drizzling

⅓ cup mayonnaise or reduced-fat mayonnaise

2 oranges, zested, and 1 orange reserved for juice

1 teaspoon ground chipotle chili powder, or ¼ to ½ teaspoon cayenne pepper

2 egg whites, beaten with a fork

1 handful fresh flat-leaf parsley, chopped

1 tablespoon Old Bay seasoning or other seafood seasoning blend

1 small red bell pepper, cored, seeded, and finely diced

Salt and freshly ground black pepper

1 pound lump crabmeat, picked over to remove shells and cartilage (available in tubs at fish counter)

½ cup panko (Japanese bread crumbs) (omit if you do not require crunch to your cakes)

2 heads Belgian endive, leaves pulled apart and chopped into large pieces

1 head radicchio, cored and thinly sliced

1 head Bibb or Boston lettuce, torn into bite-size pieces

2 tablespoons red wine vinegar

1 tablespoon honey

½ tablespoon dry mustard or 1 tablespoon prepared Dijon mustard

Preheat the oven to 375°F.

Line a baking sheet with aluminum foil and brush with a little EVOO. In a bowl combine the mayonnaise, orange zest, chipotle powder, egg whites, parsley, Old Bay seasoning, bell pepper, salt, and pepper. Add the crabmeat and gently fold the mixture together, trying not to break up the large pieces of crab. Add half of the seasoned crab mixture to the food processor. Using the pulse function, zap it 4 or 5 times. You are not trying to make a paste, you are just looking for a finer blend. Thoroughly combine the pulsed crab with the chunky crab, folding it together some-what gently so as not to break up the chunky part. With your hand, score the crab mixture into 4 equal portions. Divide each portion into 2. Scoop the portion with an ice cream scoop and release onto the baking sheet. Press down to form each of your 8 portions into a 1-inch-thick cake. If you are going for the panko bread crumbs, drizzle the panko with a little EVOO and sprinkle each cake with about 1 tablespoon of the panko. Bake the crab cakes on the top rack of the oven for 12 to 13 minutes, or until cooked through. While the crab cakes are cooking, prepare the sweet and bitter salad.

In a large salad bowl combine the endive, radicchio, and lettuce. To make the dressing, in another bowl squeeze the juice of the reserved orange, then add the red wine vinegar, honey, and mustard. Whisk in about 3 tablespoons EVOO, pouring it in a slow, steady stream. Pour the dressing over the salad and toss to coat.

Serve 2 crab cakes on top of a portion of the sweet and bitter salad.

RECIPISTORY

Since messing with a low-carb-not-no-carb lifestyle, I've been trying to figure out a way to make crab cakes hold together (I used to be the Queen of Crab Cakes when I could use lots of cracker meal and bread crumbs). Finally I hit on it! I let the crab be the binder for the crab. This is done by processing half of the crab and leaving the other half nice and chunky. Still, I missed the crunch, so I added a bare minimum of panko bread crumbs for a textured top.

Halibut with Fire-Roasted Salsa, Avocado Boats, and Jicama Slaw Salad

4 SERVINGS

JICAMA SLAW

    Zest and juice of 2 limes

    A handful of fresh cilantro, finely chopped

2 teaspoons hot sauce, such as Tabasco (eyeball it)

2 tablespoons vegetable oil (eyeball it)

1 jicama, about 1 pound

    Coarse salt

FIRE-ROASTED SALSA

1 tablespoon vegetable oil (once around the pan)

2 jalapeños

1 can diced fire-roasted tomatoes, such as Muir Glen brand, drained

2 tablespoons fresh cilantro, finely chopped

1 tablespoon fresh mint, finely chopped

¼ red onion, finely chopped

    Coarse salt

FISH

¼ cup extra-virgin olive oil (EVOO)

4 6-ounce halibut fillets

    Juice of ¼ lemon

    Salt and freshly ground black pepper

AVOCADO BOATS

2 ripe Hass avocados

    Juice of ½ lemon

    Hot sauce, about 4 teaspoons

    Coarse salt

    Extra-virgin olive oil (EVOO), for drizzling

Begin with the slaw salad. In a medium bowl, combine the lime zest and juice with the cilantro, hot sauce, and vegetable oil. With a paring knife peel the light brown skin from the jicama; slice ¼-inch-thick disks, stack the disks up, then cut into ¼-inch-wide strips. Add the jicama to the dressing and toss it around, then season with salt to taste and reserve.

To make the salsa: Heat a medium nonstick skillet over high heat. Add the veg oil and jalapeños and char until blackened on all sides. Remove the pan from the heat and remove the jalapeños to a cutting board. While the peppers cool enough to handle, in a bowl combine the fire-roasted tomatoes with the cilantro, mint, and red onion. Halve the peppers and remove the tops and seeds. Chop the jalapeño and add to the salsa. Toss to combine and season with salt to taste, then reserve.

Return the nonstick skillet to the stove with the EVOO in it and heat the oil over medium-high heat. Dress the fish with lemon juice and salt and pepper on both sides. When the oil ripples and begins to smoke, add the fish and cook for 4 minutes on each side, or until firm and opaque.

While the fish cooks, cut the avocados in half all the way down to the pit. Twist to separate the avocados. Use a spoon to remove the pits and scoop the flesh from the skin, keeping each half intact. Fill the cavity or "boat" with a little lemon juice, hot sauce, a pinch of salt, and a drizzle of EVOO.

To serve, place the fish on a dinner plate and top with the salsa. Pile some jicama alongside. Add an avocado boat to the plate and serve.

Broiled Haddock with Bacon-Fried Greens

4 SERVINGS

- 1 tablespoon extra-virgin olive oil (EVOO) (once around the pan)
- 4 slices applewood-smoked bacon, chopped
- 1 medium red onion, chopped
- 3 tablespoons red wine vinegar
- 6 cups (1½ pounds) Swiss chard or red Swiss chard, coarsely chopped
  Salt and freshly ground black pepper
- ½ teaspoon grated nutmeg (eyeball it)
- 5 tablespoons softened butter
- 2¼ to 2½ pounds haddock fillets, cut into 4 portions
  Juice of ½ lemon
- ¼ cup mayonnaise
- 10 fresh chive blades, snipped or chopped

Preheat the broiler and preheat a skillet over medium-high heat.

To the skillet, add the EVOO and bacon. Render the bacon fat 3 minutes, then add the onion and cook together with the bacon for another 3 or 4 minutes. Deglaze the pan with the vinegar. Add the greens in bunches, wilting into the pan. Season the greens with salt, pepper, and nutmeg. Reduce the heat to medium low and let the greens cook for 10 minutes, tossing occasionally with tongs.

Grease a shallow broiler pan with 1 tablespoon of the butter. Set the fish into the pan, white, fleshy side up. Dress the fish with the lemon juice and some salt. Mix the 4 tablespoons of remaining butter with the mayonnaise. Broil the fish for 3 or 4 minutes, 3 or 4 inches from heat, then remove from the oven and slather the combined mayo-butter evenly over the fish. If the pan looks dry, add a splash of water to it and return the fish to the oven. Broil the fish for 5 minutes more, or until the top of the haddock is bubbly and evenly browned. Top the cooked fish with the chives and carefully transfer to dinner plates with a fish spatula. Serve with a pile of bacon-fried greens on the side.

Seafood au Gratin with Sautéed Artichokes and Spinach

4 SERVINGS

¼ cup plus 1 tablespoon extra-virgin olive oil (EVOO)

4 tablespoons butter

1 bay leaf, fresh or dried

1½ pounds cod, cut into chunks

1 pound large raw shrimp, peeled, deveined, and tails removed, coarsely chopped

1 lemon

1 large shallot, finely chopped

2 tablespoons flour

½ cup chicken stock or broth

1 cup heavy cream

3 tablespoons dry sherry

¼ teaspoon grated nutmeg

Salt and freshly ground black pepper

3 garlic cloves, chopped

2 cans (15 ounces each) quartered artichoke hearts in water, drained

1 pound triple-washed spinach, stems discarded, coarsely chopped

2 cups (8 ounces) shredded Gruyère cheese

1 teaspoon sweet paprika

2 tablespoons chopped fresh flat-leaf parsley

2 to 3 tablespoons grated Parmigiano-Reggiano or Parmesan cheese

Preheat a broiler to high.

To a large skillet over medium heat add 1 tablespoon of the EVOO (once around the pan), 2 tablespoons of the butter, and the bay leaf. Add the fish and shrimp and cook for 2 to 3 minutes on each side, turning carefully with fish spatula. Remove the fish and shrimp to a plate, squeeze lemon juice on the cooked fish, and reserve. Add 2 tablespoons more butter to the pan and the

continued ....➤

shallot. Sauté the shallot for 2 minutes, then add the flour and cook another minute. Whisk in the stock and thicken for a minute. Add the cream to the sauce and bring to a bubble. Stir in the sherry, then season the sauce with nutmeg, salt, and pepper. Slide the seafood back into the pan and cook together over medium-low heat to reduce the sauce and finish cooking the seafood, 5 to 6 minutes.

Heat a second skillet over medium-high heat. Add the remaining EVOO, the garlic, and drained artichokes. Fry for 2 minutes, then wilt in the spinach and season with salt and pepper to taste. Turn the pan off and reserve.

Pour the seafood into a shallow casserole and top with the Gruyère cheese, paprika, parsley, and Parm. Brown the casserole and serve. Pile the spinach and artichokes alongside the seafood.

Smoked Salmon with All the Trimmings and Crushed Cherry Tomato Vinaigrette

When you are too exhausted to move, this simple supper stands you back up. Actually, it makes a nice Sunday brunch or late-night snack as well and can easily be adjusted to feed from one to some.

4 SERVINGS

- 6 eggs
- ½ pint cherry tomatoes, cut in half
- 2 tablespoons sherry vinegar or red wine vinegar
- 2 tablespoons extra-virgin olive oil (EVOO)
  Salt and freshly ground black pepper
- 8 large slices good-quality smoked salmon
- 1 bunch arugula, washed and trimmed of thick stems

1 bunch watercress, washed and trimmed of thick stems
1 head Belgian endive, chopped
¼ cup chopped fresh flat-leaf parsley
½ English (seedless) cucumber (the one wrapped in plastic), diced
½ small red onion, thinly sliced
1½ tablespoons capers, drained

Place the eggs in a small saucepot and add enough water to cover. Set over high heat and bring up to a simmer. Once the eggs are at a simmer, turn the heat off, cover with a lid, and let sit for 10 minutes. Drain the eggs of the hot water and then aggressively shake the pan to crack the eggshells. Run the eggs under cold water until they've cooled down. Peel the shells from the eggs. Set the eggs aside.

While the eggs are cooking, make the crushed cherry tomato dressing. Add the cherry tomatoes to a bowl along with the sherry vinegar, EVOO, and salt and pepper to taste. With a fork, crush the cherry tomatoes a little bit. Reserve the dressing.

Place two slices of salmon on four serving plates. Don't overlap the salmon; you want it to cover as much of the bottom of the plate as possible. In a large bowl combine the arugula, watercress, endive, parsley, cucumber, red onion, and capers. Cut the cooled hard-boiled eggs into quarters and add to the vegetables in the bowl. Gently toss, trying not to break up the eggs too much. Place a serving of the salad in the center of the plated salmon. Mix up the reserved cherry tomato dressing with your fork, then distribute it among the 4 plates.

Mariel's Sauce for "Mish"

I have a very beautiful friend, Mariel Hemingway. She eats all organic foods, only fish, no meat, and she includes no carbs whatsoever in her diet. She makes a double dinner every night: one for her, one for the fam. However, when she makes this one really crazy blender sauce, it gets passed to everyone. (Mariel makes half of her food for each day in a blender.) The sauce is awesome with chicken, pork, meat, or fish. This is my version of her specialty. I call it Mariel's Sauce for "Mish"—meat or fish.

4 SERVINGS

- 3 tablespoons red wine vinegar
- 3 tablespoons pitted kalamata olives
- A pinch of Stevia or Splenda (no-carb sweetener) or a drip of honey
- 1/2 cup yellow mustard (Mariel likes French's brand)
- 2 cups spinach leaves, coarsely chopped
- 1 cup (about 20 leaves) basil
- 1/4 cup extra-virgin olive oil (EVOO) (eyeball it)
- Salt and freshly ground black pepper

In a blender combine the vinegar, olives, no-carb sweetener or a drip of honey, mustard, spinach, and basil. Blend on high speed and stream in the EVOO. Season with salt and pepper.

Lemon Lamb Chops with Lentils and Radishes

4 SERVINGS

- 1 cup lentils, French green or brown
- 3 tablespoons fresh thyme leaves
- Zest of 2 lemons
- 2 garlic cloves, smashed out of its skin
- 2 teaspoons coarse salt
- 1 teaspoon coarse black pepper
- Extra-virgin olive oil (EVOO), for drizzling
- 8 loin lamb chops
- 2 tablespoons butter
- 2 shallots, thinly sliced
- 6 radishes, thinly sliced
- Salt and freshly ground black pepper
- 3 tablespoons sherry vinegar
- ¼ cup chopped fresh dill
- ¼ cup fresh flat-leaf parsley (a couple of handfuls)

Boil the lentils in a medium pot in 2 inches of water for 20 minutes.

Preheat the broiler. Combine the thyme, lemon zest, and garlic on a cutting board. Chop together, then add the salt and pepper and mash with the flat of the knife. Drizzle EVOO over the chops. Rub them with the herb and garlic mixture and arrange on a slotted broiler pan. Broil the chops 6 to 8 inches from heat for 5 minutes on each side for medium doneness. Allow the meat to rest 5 minutes.

Heat a medium skillet over medium heat and add the butter. Melt the butter and add the shallots. Sauté for 3 minutes. Add the radishes to the skillet and coat in the butter and shallots. Drain the lentils. Add them to the skillet and season with salt and pepper. Add the vinegar, dill, and parsley. Taste and adjust the seasonings.

Pile the lentils and radishes on plates and serve up 2 chops per person.

Rosemary-Lemon Broiled Lamb Chops with Gremolata and White Beans, Prosciutto, and Greens

4 SERVINGS

- 4 small sprigs or 1 long stem fresh rosemary, needles removed then finely chopped (3 tablespoons)
  Zest and juice of 2 lemons
- 5 tablespoons extra-virgin olive oil (EVOO), divided
- 4 garlic cloves, chopped, divided
- 8 loin lamb chops
  Salt and freshly ground black pepper
- ¼ cup fresh flat-leaf parsley (a handful)
- 1 teaspoon crushed hot red pepper flakes
- 1 small yellow onion, chopped
- 1 can (15 ounces) cannellini beans, drained, well rinsed, and shaken dry
- 1 bunch arugula, washed and trimmed of thick stems
- ¼ pound sliced prosciutto, cut into strips

Preheat the broiler to high.

In a shallow dish combine the rosemary, lemon juice, about 3 tablespoons of the EVOO, and one quarter of the chopped garlic. Add the lamb chops and rub the mixture on to both sides of all the chops. Season the chops with salt and pepper and arrange the chops on a broiler pan. Place the chops about 6 to 8 inches from the broiler and cook for 5 minutes on each side. Remove the chops from the broiler and let rest for 5 minutes. While the chops are cooking, prepare the gremolata.

Make a pile on your cutting board of the lemon zest, one quarter of the chopped garlic, and parsley leaves. Run your knife through the pile until well combined and finely chopped; reserve.

After you prepare the gremolata, move on to the white beans, prosciutto, and greens. Preheat a large skillet with the remaining 2 tablespoons of EVOO (twice around the pan). Add the remaining chopped garlic, the red pepper flakes, and onion. Cook for 2 minutes, then add the cannellini beans, salt, and pepper. Stir to combine and continue to cook for 3 minutes. Turn the heat off and fold in the arugula and prosciutto.

To serve, divide the cannellini bean mixture among 4 plates, and top that with 2 chops on each portion. Top each chop with a sprinkle of the gremolata.

MYOTO: MAKE YOUR OWN TAKEOUT

Move-it-Along Pork and Veggie Stir-Fry

4 SERVINGS

- 2 pounds boneless pork rib chops or loin chops, cut into thin strips
- ¼ cup tamari (dark aged soy sauce)
-   2-inch piece fresh gingerroot, peeled and grated or minced
-   Juice of 2 limes
- 1 tablespoon honey
- 3 tablespoons vegetable oil
- 1 bunch scallions, white and green parts thinly sliced and kept separate
- 4 garlic cloves, chopped
- 1 small red bell pepper, cored, seeded, and cut into strips
- 2 Anaheim peppers, cut into strips
- 1 cup shredded carrots (bagged in the produce aisle)
- 12 button mushrooms, trimmed of stems, caps thinly sliced
- ½ head broccoli, cut into very small flowerets
- ½ small head napa cabbage, core removed and leaves thinly sliced
- 1 cup chicken stock or broth
- 1 handful fresh cilantro leaves, chopped

continued ························➤

Combine the pork in a shallow dish with the tamari, ginger, half the lime juice, and honey. Let the pork marinate while you chop up all of your vegetables. By the time you are finished, the pork will have marinated long enough.

Heat a large nonstick skillet with about 2 tablespoons of the vegetable oil. Remove the pork from the marinade; shake off the excess marinade and reserve. Once the skillet is screaming hot, add the pork slices in one even layer. Cook the sliced pork without stirring for 2 minutes. Toss the pork with tongs and cook for 1 more minute. Remove the pork from the pan and reserve. Add the remaining tablespoon of vegetable oil to the skillet. Add the white part of the scallions, the garlic, and the bell pepper, Anaheim peppers, shredded carrots, and mushrooms. Cook for 1 minute, stirring frequently. Add the broccoli and the napa cabbage; continue to cook and stir for 2 minutes. Add the reserved marinade and the chicken stock, bring up to a simmer, and cook for 2 minutes. Add the pork back to the skillet and cook for 1 more minute, or until the pork is cooked through. Turn the heat off, add the remaining lime juice and the cilantro, and toss to distribute. Taste for seasoning, add more tamari or lime juice accordingly, and serve immediately.

Cacio e Pepe (Cheese and Pepper) Spaghetti Squash

Pork Loin Chops with Sweet and Hot Peppers

Wilted Spinach with Garlic Chips

Cacio e Pepe (Cheese and Pepper) Spaghetti Squash

While the squash cooks, work on the chops (recipe follows).

4 SERVINGS

- 1 4-pound spaghetti squash
- 2 tablespoons extra-virgin olive oil (EVOO)
- 1 cup grated Romano cheese
  Salt and lots of coarse ground black pepper

To microwave squash: Cut in half and seed. Place ¼ inch water in a microwave-safe dish. Place the squash in the dish, the cut sides down—the sides will overlap. Cover with plastic wrap and microwave on High for 13 minutes. Reserve ¼ cup of the cooking liquid in a bowl. Shred the squash and add the "spaghetti" to the bowl with the reserved liquid.

To boil squash: Cut in half and seed. Boil the squash until tender, 15 to 20 minutes. Place ¼ cup, a ladleful, of cooking water into a bowl, then drain and shred the squash. Transfer to the bowl with the reserved liquid.

Toss the squash with the reserved liquid and dress with EVOO, lots of cheese, salt to taste, and lots of black pepper and serve.

Pork Loin Chops with Sweet and Hot Peppers

While the chops are cooking, work on the Wilted Spinach with Garlic Chips, opposite.

4 SERVINGS

- 4 center-cut pork loin chops, 1 inch thick
  Salt and freshly ground black pepper
- 2 tablespoons extra-virgin olive oil (EVOO)
- 1 yellow bell pepper, cored, seeded, and sliced
- 1 orange bell pepper, cored, seeded, and sliced
- 4 jarred red hot Italian cherry peppers, sliced
- 1/2 cup white wine or chicken stock
- 2 tablespoons chopped fresh flat-leaf parsley (a handful)

Heat a large skillet over medium-high heat. Season the chops with salt and pepper. Add 1 tablespoon of the EVOO to the pan (once around the pan). Add the chops and cook for 5 minutes on each side.

After the chops have cooked through, transfer to a platter and cover with foil. Return the pan to heat and add the remaining tablespoon of EVOO and the bell peppers. Sauté the peppers, stirring frequently, for 5 minutes. Add the hot cherry peppers and a splash of their brine to the pan, and cook for 1 minute. Add the wine or stock and scrape up the pan drippings. Arrange the peppers over the chops and sprinkle with parsley. Serve with the spinach and the cacio e pepe spaghetti squash.

Wilted Spinach with Garlic Chips

4 SERVINGS

- 1/4 cup extra-virgin olive oil (EVOO) (4 times around the pan)
- 4 large garlic cloves, carefully peeled and very thinly sliced into chips
- 2 pounds triple-washed spinach, stems removed
- 1/2 teaspoon grated nutmeg
  Coarse salt and coarse black pepper

Place a large skillet on the stove and add the oil and garlic chips. Turn heat onto low and let the garlic chips fry up until golden, flipping them around from time to time, about 5 minutes. Remove the crisp garlic chips with a slotted spoon and reserve. Add the spinach to the pan, turning with tongs to wilt it all in. Season the spinach with the nutmeg, salt, and pepper. Serve immediately, garnished with the garlic chips.

"Stuffed" Pork Chops with Sausage and Apricots

4 SERVINGS

8	thin-cut, boneless pork loin chops
	Salt and freshly ground black pepper
3	tablespoons extra-virgin olive oil (EVOO)
2	cups chicken stock or broth
1	pound Italian bulk sausage
3	celery ribs, chopped
1	medium onion, chopped
½	red bell pepper, cored, seeded, and chopped
6	dried apricots, chopped
¼	cup chopped fresh flat-leaf parsley
2	tablespoons chopped fresh sage
2	tablespoons butter
1	tablespoon flour (it's only a tablespoon, get over it!)
½	cup heavy cream
	A pinch of nutmeg, grated or ground

Preheat a large skillet over medium-high heat. Preheat the oven to 350°F.

Season the chops with salt and pepper. Add 2 tablespoons of the EVOO to the hot skillet, then add the chops to sear and caramelize the meat on each side, a minute or two. Transfer the chops to a pan or casserole dish and add about $\frac{1}{2}$ cup of the chicken stock to help the meat remain moist while it finishes cooking—just eyeball the amount. Loosely cover the dish or pan with foil before placing in the oven.

Start the Sautéed Yellow Squash, page 146, then move back to the stuffing in this recipe.

Return the skillet to the stove and add the remaining tablespoon of EVOO. Add the sausage and crumble it as it browns. Add the celery and onion and cook for 2 or 3 minutes, then add the bell pepper and apricots. Cook for 2 minutes, then add the parsley and sage and another $\frac{1}{2}$ cup chicken broth. Reduce the heat and cook the stuffing for 5 or 6 minutes longer, until the apricots are tender and plump. Remove the stuffing to a small bowl, scraping the pan free of as much food as possible, then return the same skillet to moderate heat. Add the butter to the skillet. When the butter melts, add the flour and whisk. Cook the flour with the butter for 1 minute, then add the remaining cup of broth. Bring both to a bubble, then stir in the heavy cream—eyeball it. Bring the gravy to a bubble. Add a pinch of nutmeg and black pepper and simmer for 5 minutes to thicken a bit.

To serve, remove the chops from oven. Place 4 chops on individual plates or on a platter. Mound the sausage and vegetables on the chops, then top each with a second chop and pour gravy down over the top of stacked chops and stuffing. The pan drippings may also be added to the gravy to stretch the amount.

Sautéed Yellow Squash

4 SERVINGS

- 1 tablespoon extra-virgin olive oil (EVOO)
- 2 tablespoons butter
- 1/2 red bell pepper, cored, seeded, and chopped
- 2 small to medium yellow squash, sliced
  Salt and freshly ground black pepper
- 2 tablespoons chopped fresh flat-leaf parsley
- 2 tablespoons chives or 2 scallions, chopped (optional)

Preheat a skillet over medium-high heat. Add the EVOO, then the butter. When the butter melts, add the bell pepper and squash. Sauté for 12 minutes, or until the squash is tender. Add salt and pepper to taste and the parsley. Add the chives or scallions if you would like a layer of light onion flavor on the dish as well.

Pork Chops in Spiced-Apple Pan Sauce with Roasted Broccoli Spears

4 SERVINGS

- 1 large head or 2 small heads broccoli
- 3 garlic cloves, chopped
  Salt and freshly ground black pepper
- 2 tablespoons extra-virgin olive oil (EVOO), plus some for drizzling
- 4 boneless pork loin or rib chops, 1 1/2 inches thick
- 2 tablespoons butter
- 1 Spanish onion, thinly sliced

2 tablespoons fresh thyme leaves, stripped from 4 or 5 sprigs, chopped
1 Granny Smith apple, cored and thinly sliced
2 pinches ground nutmeg or fresh grated nutmeg (about ¼ teaspoon)
1 teaspoon ground cinnamon
1 cup chicken stock or broth
  A handful fresh flat-leaf parsley, chopped
  Juice of 1 lemon

Preheat the oven to 400°F.

Trim the very end off of the broccoli stems. With a peeler or a paring knife, remove the thick fibrous outer layer of the broccoli stems all the way up to within an inch of where the broccoli shoots off into its florets. Cut the broccoli lengthwise into large spears. On a baking sheet, toss the broccoli spears with the garlic, salt, pepper, and a generous drizzle of EVOO. Place the broccoli in the oven and roast for 15 minutes. The florets become brown and crispy and a little nutty tasting. YUMMO!

While the broccoli is roasting, preheat a large skillet over high heat with 2 tablespoons of EVOO (twice around the pan). Liberally season the pork chops with salt and pepper and sear on both sides for 2 minutes, or until they are golden brown. Remove the chops from the skillet and reserve. Add the butter to the pork skillet, add the onion, thyme, sliced apple, nutmeg, and cinnamon. Cook, stirring frequently, for 3 to 5 minutes, or until the onion and apples are tender. Add the chicken stock and bring up to a simmer. Add the pork chops back to the pan and cook for 5 to 7 minutes longer, or until the chops are cooked through. Add the parsley and lemon juice to the chops and stir to distribute.

Serve the chops topped with the spiced-apple pan sauce alongside the roasted broccoli spears.

Sliced Pork Tenderloin Saltimbocca on Spinach and Arugula Salad

4 SERVINGS

- 2 pork tenderloins (about 2 pounds), trimmed of silver skin and connective tissue
- 6 garlic cloves, peeled
- ¼ cup extra-virgin olive oil (EVOO), plus more for drizzling
  Salt and freshly ground black pepper
  A bundle of fresh sage leaves
- ¼ pound prosciutto di Parma
- 1 pound baby spinach
- 2 cups arugula leaves (1 bunch), washed and trimmed of stems
- 6 button mushrooms, trimmed and thinly sliced
- 1 shallot, minced
- 2 tablespoons red wine vinegar
  Juice of ½ lemon
- 2 tablespoons fresh chopped thyme leaves

Preheat the oven to 450°F.

Place the pork tenderloins on a baking sheet lined with aluminum foil. Cut 3 slits into each loin a few inches apart. Nest the cloves of garlic into the slits. Slather the pork with a healthy drizzle of EVOO and use your hands to coat the pork. Strap leaves of sage across each piece of pork. Wrap the tenderloins in prosciutto, covering the pork entirely. Drizzle again with EVOO. Roast the pork for 25 minutes. While the pork roasts, prepare the salad.

Combine the greens and mushrooms in a salad bowl. In a smaller bowl, combine the minced shallot with the vinegar, lemon juice, and thyme. Let stand for 15 minutes. (Nice place for a red wine break here. Even Atkins himself had a glass now and again.) Stream about ¼ cup of EVOO into the dressing while whisking to emulsify it. Toss the salad with the dressing.

To serve, pile the salad onto plates. Slice the tenderloins on an angle, ½-inch slices, and arrange the sliced pork atop the salad.

Lemon Roast Pork Tenderloins with Warm Beets, Chicory, and Goat Cheese

4 SERVINGS

- 4 tablespoons extra-virgin olive oil (EVOO), divided
- 1 tablespoon dry mustard or 2 tablespoons prepared Dijon mustard
- 3 garlic cloves, chopped
  Juice and zest of 2 lemons
- 2 pork tenderloins (2 to 2¼ pounds), trimmed of silver skin and connective tissue
  Salt and freshly ground black pepper
- 4 slices bacon, chopped
- 1 small yellow onion, thinly sliced
- 1 tablespoon fresh thyme leaves, chopped
- 1 can (15 ounces) sliced beets, drained of all but about 4 tablespoons juice
- 1 head chicory, washed, dried, and torn into bite-size pieces (see Tidbit, page 150)
- 20 fresh basil leaves, chopped
- 1 handful fresh flat-leaf parsley, chopped
- ½ cup crumbled goat cheese

Preheat the oven to 450°F.

In a small bowl combine 2 tablespoons of the EVOO, the mustard, garlic, and half the lemon juice and reserve. Toss the tender-

continued ....

loins in the lemon mixture. Place the tenderloins on a nonstick baking sheet with a rim. Season them with salt and pepper and roast for 25 minutes, then remove and let rest.

While the pork is roasting, preheat a medium-size skillet with the remaining 2 tablespoons of EVOO over medium-high heat. Add the chopped bacon and cook until crisp, about 3 minutes. Add the onion and thyme and cook for 2 to 3 minutes, stirring occasionally. Add the sliced beets and the reserved beet juice, salt, and pepper and cook for 2 more minutes, or until the beets are warmed through.

Meanwhile, in a salad bowl combine the chicory, lemon zest, the remaining lemon juice, the basil, and parsley. Transfer the warm beets to the salad bowl and toss to combine and wilt the chicory.

Slice the pork thin on an angle. Serve the sliced pork with the warm beets and chicory alongside. Top the warm vegetables with goat cheese crumbles.

TIDBIT

Chicory is great raw or cooked. It has a big flavor that trumps regular lettuce any day.

Lower-Carb Cocktail Party Snack Menu

Crab Salad Bites on Endive, Baby Lamb Chops with
Artichoke and Tarragon Dip, and Ham and Cheese Mini
Frittatas (page 18)

above left
Ginger-Garlic Tuna Burgers on Cucumber Salad with Salted Edamame (page 50)

above
Mexican Fondue (page 67)

left
Lemon, Garlic, and Cilantro Baked Stuffed Tomatoes (page 73)

right
Cream of Cheddar Soup and Lime Chicken Avocado Salad (page 122)

left

Sesame-Crusted Red Snapper with Ginger-Dressed Snappy Veggies (page 125)

below

Low-Carb Roman Feast
Cacio e Pepe Spaghetti Squash (page 141), Pork Loin Chops with Sweet and Hot Peppers (page 142), and Wilted Spinach with Garlic Chips (page 143)

opposite

Lower Carbs, Higher Marks, Gourmet for Every Day Dinner
Prosciutto-Wrapped Endive and Radicchio with Balsamic-Fig Reduction (page 193) and Hazelnut-Crusted Chicken with Gorgonzola Sauce (page 194)

opposite

Things-to-Thank-the-Swedes-for-Menu
Red Radish, Red Apple and Red Onion Salad
(page 230) and Swedish Meatballs on Noodles
(page 231)

above

Mascarpone Parfait with Citrus Salad (page 236)

left

Ginger-Poached Pears with Ricotta and
Blueberries (page 235)

Very Berry Crumble (page 237)

Chili-Rubbed Roast Pork Tenderloins with Crunchy, Chunky Black Bean and Jicama Salad

4 SERVINGS

- 2 pork tenderloins (2 to 2¼ pounds), trimmed of silver skin and connective tissue
- 2 tablespoons chili powder
- 1 tablespoon ground cumin
  Salt and freshly ground black pepper
- 4 tablespoons extra-virgin olive oil (EVOO), plus more for drizzling
  Juice of 2 limes
- 1 tablespoon Dijon mustard
- 1 jicama (1 pound)
- 1 ripe Hass avocado
- 1 small red onion, thinly sliced
- 1 English (seedless) cucumber (the one wrapped in plastic), cut into ¼-inch-thick disks
- 1 can (15 ounces) black beans, drained and thoroughly rinsed
  A handful of fresh cilantro, chopped
  A handful of fresh flat-leaf parsley, chopped

Preheat the oven to 450°F.

Place the tenderloins on a nonstick baking sheet with a rim. Combine the chili powder and cumin in a small bowl. Rub the seasoning mixture into the tenderloins, coating them completely. Season with some salt and pepper and then drizzle the tenderloins with EVOO, just enough to coat. Roast for 25 minutes. Allow the meat to rest. While the pork is roasting, prepare the black bean and jicama salad.

In a small bowl combine the lime juice, mustard, salt, and pepper. Whisk in about 4 tablespoons EVOO. With a paring knife, peel

continued ....➤

the light brown skin from the jicama. Slice it into ¼-inch-thick disks, stack the disks up, then cut into ¼-inch-wide strips and reserve. Cut all around the circumference of the ripe avocado, lengthwise and down to the pit. Twist and separate the halved fruit. Remove the pit with a spoon, then scoop the flesh out in one piece from both halves. Chop the avocado into bite-size pieces. In a salad bowl combine the jicama, avocado chunks, red onion, cucumber, black beans, cilantro, and parsley. Pour the dressing over the salad and toss to combine.

Slice the pork on an angle into ½-inch-thick slices. Serve the sliced pork with the salad piled on top.

TIDBIT
Jicama tastes both sweet and nutty, and the thing I love about it is that it is really crispy. I love it in all kinds of salads.

TIDBIT
This mustard butter (opposite) is great on more than just pork; try it on steaks and chicken, and even finish off some sautéed veggies with it.

Pork Chops Slathered in Mustard Butter with Bacon-Braised Napa

4 SERVINGS

- 4 tablespoons extra virgin olive oil (EVOO)
- 6 slices center-cut or applewood-smoked bacon, chopped
- 3 garlic cloves, chopped
- 1 medium Spanish onion, thinly sliced
- 2 tablespoons fresh thyme leaves, 4 or 5 sprigs stripped, chopped
- 1 small head napa cabbage, cored and sliced (1¼ pounds)
  Salt and freshly ground black pepper
- ¼ cup plus a splash cider vinegar
- ½ cup (2 ounces) golden raisins (a couple of handfuls)
- ¾ cup chicken stock
- 4 center-cut loin pork chops or rib chops, 1 inch thick
- 4 tablespoons butter, very soft
- 2 tablespoons grainy mustard
- 2 tablespoons fresh chopped flat-leaf parsley

Heat a large skillet over medium-high heat with 2 tablespoons of the EVOO (twice around the pan). Add the bacon and cook until crisp, 3 minutes. Add the garlic, onion, and thyme and cook for 1 minute. Add the cabbage, salt, and pepper, toss to combine, then add ¼ cup of the cider vinegar, the raisins, and the chicken stock. Turn down the heat to medium and continue to cook for 8 to 10 minutes, stirring occasionally.

While the cabbage is cooking, heat another large skillet over medium-high heat with the remaining 2 tablespoons of EVOO. Liberally season the pork chops with salt and pepper. Add the chops and cook for 5 minutes on each side.

For the mustard butter, in a small bowl combine the soft butter, grainy mustard, chopped parsley, and a splash of cider vinegar. Top each chop with a heaping tablespoon of the mustard butter and serve alongside the bacon-braised cabbage.

Meatball and Spinach No-sagna and a Basic-Is-Best Italian Salad

This meat and spinach casserole hits the same flavor notes as lasagna, hold the noodles: No-sagna Lasagna! Serve it with a simple salad of mixed greens.

4 SERVINGS

MEATBALLS

- 1½ pounds ground sirloin
- 1 large egg, beaten
- ½ cup Italian bread crumbs (see Tidbit)
- ½ yellow onion, chopped
- 4 garlic cloves, crushed and finely chopped
- ¼ cup fresh flat-leaf parsley (a fistful of leaves), chopped
- ½ cup grated Parmigiano or Romano (a couple of generous handfuls)
  Salt and freshly ground black pepper
- 2 tablespoons extra-virgin olive oil (EVOO) (twice around the pan)
- 1 teaspoon crushed hot red pepper flakes
- 1 can (14 ounces) chunky-style crushed tomatoes
- 2½ cups (10 ounces) shredded provolone cheese or Italian four-cheese blend

SPINACH

- 2 tablespoons extra-virgin olive oil (EVOO) (twice around the pan)
- ½ yellow onion, chopped
  Salt and freshly ground black pepper
- 2 10-ounce boxes chopped spinach, defrosted
- ½ cup chicken stock or broth
- ½ cup heavy cream
  A generous grating of fresh nutmeg or ¼ teaspoon ground
- ½ cup fresh basil leaves, for garnish

Preheat the broiler.

Place the ground sirloin in a large mixing bowl and punch a well into the center of the meat. Fill the well with the egg, bread crumbs, onion, half of the chopped garlic, half of the parsley, the

Parmigiano or Romano cheese, and a little salt and pepper. Mix the meatball ingredients until well combined yet not overmixed. Divide into 4 equal parts, then roll each part into 5 balls. Heat a large nonstick skillet over medium-high heat with the EVOO. Add the meatballs and brown on all sides, about 5 minutes. Scoot the meatballs to the side of the skillet and add the remaining garlic and the red pepper flakes. Cook for 1 minute. Add the tomatoes, mix to combine. Shake the skillet to coat the meatballs in the sauce and simmer for 5 to 6 minutes more. While the meatballs are simmering, start the spinach.

Heat a medium-size skillet over medium-high heat with the EVOO. Add the onion, salt, and pepper. Cook for 1 minute. While the onion is cooking, transfer the defrosted spinach to a clean kitchen towel and wring all the liquid out. Add the spinach, chicken stock, and cream to the skillet. Season with nutmeg and cook for 2 minutes or until the mixture is thick. Spread the spinach mixture over the bottom of a baking dish. Top with the meatballs and the tomato sauce. Top that with the shredded provolone or Italian four-cheese blend. Place under the preheated broiler about 6 inches from the heat to melt and evenly brown the cheese, about 3 minutes.

Remove the no-sagna from the broiler and garnish with lots of torn or shredded basil.

TIDBIT

You can omit the bread crumbs if you are feeling hard-core no-carb. The texture of the meatballs will be a little different but the flavor will still be great.

Beef Stroganoff over Buttered Parsley-Cauliflower "Noodles"

If you are looking to save a few bucks and a little time, you can buy 2 pounds of pepper steak strips and cut that into bite-size pieces. The beef won't be quite as tender but the flavor will be great.

4 SERVINGS

- 4 tablespoons vegetable oil
- 2 pounds beef tenderloin
  Salt and freshly ground black pepper
- 5 tablespoons butter
- 1 small onion, sliced
- 2 tablespoons flour
- 2 cans (about 3 cups total) beef consommé
- 2 tablespoons Dijon mustard
- 1 small head cauliflower
- ½ cup chicken stock or broth
- ¾ cup chopped fresh flat-leaf parsley, divided
- 1 cup sour cream
- 6 cornichons or baby gherkins, chopped (optional)

Fill a large skillet with 1 inch of water. Place the skillet over high heat and bring to a boil for the cauliflower "noodles."

Preheat a large skillet with 2 tablespoons of the vegetable oil (twice around the pan) over high heat. You will be searing the meat in this pan, so you want it to be screaming hot.

Thinly slice the meat and cut into 2-inch-long very thin strips. Season the meat with salt and pepper and add to the hot oil, spreading the meat out in an even layer. Sear the meat, caramelizing it, for about 2 minutes without touching it, then toss and continue to cook for another 2 minutes.

Remove the meat from the pan and reserve on a plate. Reduce heat on the burner to medium low. Cool the pan for a minute, then add 2 tablespoons of the butter to the skillet, melt, and add half of the sliced onion. Cook for 2 to 3 minutes, then add the flour, stirring to distribute. Cook the flour for 30 seconds. Whisk in the beef consommé and the Dijon mustard and turn the heat down to low, gently simmering for 10 minutes.

While the stroganoff sauce is cooking, prepare the cauliflower "noodles": With a paring knife, remove the stem of the cauliflower, trying to keep the head intact. With the cut side down on the cutting board, slice the cauliflower into ¼-inch-thick slices. Stack those slices and cut them in half, lengthwise. Add some salt and the cauliflower "noodles" to the skillet with the boiling water. Cook for 2 minutes. Drain the cauliflower in a colander. Return the pan to the heat and add the remaining 2 tablespoons of vegetable oil, the remaining onion, salt, and pepper; cook for 1 minute.

Add the cauliflower and chicken stock to the onion, stir to coat, and cook for 3 minutes, or until the cauliflower is tender. Turn the heat off and add the remaining 3 tablespoons of butter and ½ cup of the chopped parsley. Toss to coat and reserve while you finish off the stroganoff.

Add the meat back to the pan with the stroganoff sauce. Add the sour cream, stirring to combine. Turn the heat back up to medium high and simmer for 2 to 3 minutes, to finish cooking the meat. Taste the dish, checking for seasoning, and arrange the beef stroganoff on a bed of the cauliflower "noodles." Garnish with the remaining ¼ cup chopped parsley and the chopped cornichons.

TIDBIT

For easy slicing of raw meat, pop it into the freezer for 10 to 15 minutes before starting to prepare the meal. This firms up the meat and you'll find that it will be easier to control the thickness of the slices.

London Broil with Steak Sauce Gravy, Smashed Cauliflower with Cheese, and Red Chard with Ham

4 SERVINGS

1 large head cauliflower, cut into florets

1 cup chicken stock or broth

4 tablespoons butter, cut into pieces

1 cup shredded white extra-sharp Vermont Cheddar cheese, such as Cabot brand

¼ cup grated Parmigiano-Reggiano (a couple of handfuls)

Salt and coarse black pepper

A generous grating of nutmeg

1½ pounds shoulder steak, 1½ inches thick, for London broil

1 tablespoon Worcestershire sauce

2 tablespoons vegetable oil or olive oil (twice around the pan)

½ pound ham, chopped

6 cups chopped red chard (1 large bunch)

3 tablespoons red wine vinegar (eyeball it)

1 tablespoon honey

1 shallot, finely chopped

2 tablespoons flour

2 cups beef stock or broth

¼ cup steak sauce, such as A.1. or Lea and Perrins brands

Place the cauliflower in a medium shallow pot or pan. Add the stock, cover, and place the pot over high heat. When the liquid boils, reduce the heat to medium low and simmer, covered, for 8 minutes. Start the steak (see below) while the cauliflower cooks. After 8 minutes, remove the cover, raise the heat to medium high, and allow the broth and vegetable juices to reduce by half, 1 to 2 minutes. Add 2 tablespoons of the butter and the cheeses and smash the cauliflower with a masher to the same consistency as desired for mashed potatoes. Season the cauliflower with salt, pepper, and nutmeg to taste.

Turn the broiler on. Brush the meat with Worcestershire and season with salt and pepper. Broil the steak on the top rack for 6 minutes on each side, for medium-rare to medium doneness.

While the steak and cauliflower cook, heat a second large skillet over medium-high heat. Add the oil and the ham. Sear the ham and caramelize at edges, 2 minutes.

Add the chard and wilt the greens into the pan, then season with salt, pepper, and a dash of nutmeg, if you like. Cook 5 to 7 minutes more, turning frequently with tongs, then add the vinegar to the pan and a drizzle of honey. Turn to coat the greens, adjust seasoning, and transfer to a serving dish.

Remove the meat from the broiler and let it rest 5 minutes under a foil tent.

Place a small skillet over medium heat. Melt the remaining 2 tablespoons of butter, add the shallot, and cook for 2 minutes, then whisk in the flour and cook for 1 minute. Add the beef stock to the pan and bring to a bubble. Reduce the stock for 2 minutes, then add the steak sauce and black pepper, to taste.

Very thinly slice the meat on an angle against the grain (the lines in the meat). The degree of thinness will determine how tender it is to cut and chew, so make sure the carving knife is sharp—the thinner the better!

Serve the sliced steak with the steak sauce gravy all over it and the smashed cauliflower and red chard with ham piled up alongside the meat.

TIDBIT

London broil is a method of cooking, not a cut. You'll find both shoulder steak and top round packaged as "London Broil" and either works, but I prefer the shoulder cut. Bottom line: Both are cheap and very tasty if you cut them right.

Sliced Steak with Chimichurri and Baked Stuffed Tomatoes

4 SERVINGS

- 2 beefsteak tomatoes
  Salt and freshly ground black pepper
- 1 cup whole-milk ricotta cheese
- 1½ cups fresh flat-leaf parsley, chopped
- 1 cup (about 20 leaves) basil, chopped
- 4 garlic cloves, chopped
- ¾ cup grated Parmigiano-Reggiano
- 1 egg yolk
- 2 pounds boneless shoulder steak (sometimes labeled London Broil in the supermarket)
- 3 tablespoons extra-virgin olive oil (EVOO), plus some for drizzling
- ½ cup red wine vinegar or aged sherry vinegar
- 2 tablespoons fresh oregano or marjoram, chopped

Preheat the oven to 450°F.

For the baked stuffed tomatoes, make 4 tomato cups out of your 2 tomatoes. To do so, cut a very thin slice off both ends of each of the 2 tomatoes. This is to create 4 flat bottoms. Next, cut each tomato in half across its circumference. You should have 4 cup shapes, using the thinly sliced side as the bottom of the cups. Using a melon-ball scoop, remove the seeds and guts from the wide, fleshy side of each tomato, creating a tomato cup. You don't have to be too fussy about this; you are just trying to create enough room to hold the filling. When scooping, take some care not to puncture through the bottoms of the cups. If you do, don't worry, it is not the end of the world, just keep moving forward. The ripped cup will just be tricky to handle to transfer to plates later. So, next, season the inside of the tomato cavities with salt and pepper. Reserve the seasoned tomato cups while you make the filling.

In a small mixing bowl combine the ricotta cheese, half of the parsley, the basil, half of the garlic, and the cheese, and season the mixture with salt and pepper. Taste the filling and adjust the seasoning. Once you are happy with it, add the egg yolk and mix thoroughly. Divide the filling among the 4 tomato cups. Arrange in a baking dish and bake for 15 to 17 minutes. Remove the tomatoes from the oven and raise the temperature to broil.

Season the steak liberally with salt and pepper. Drizzle EVOO on both sides and place on a broiler pan. Arrange the pan under the broiler on the rack closest to the flame. Broil for 6 minutes per side. Remove from the heat to a platter, tent with a piece of foil, and allow the meat to rest for a few minutes.

While the steak is cooking, assemble the chimichurri. In a small bowl combine the vinegar, oregano or marjoram, the remaining garlic, and the remaining parsley. Season the mixture with salt and a generous amount of black pepper. Whisk in about 3 tablespoons of EVOO.

To serve, thinly slice the rested steak against the grain. Give a little mix to the chimichurri and drizzle it on top of the steak. Serve alongside the baked stuffed tomatoes.

TIDBIT

Chimichurri is an herb and vinegar condiment from Argentina, where a steak is considered naked without it. It is used with the same "got-to-have-it" conviction as mustard is on a hot dog in the USA. It tastes great on everything grilled: beef, chicken, pork, and fish. Save any leftovers or, if you are like me, make extra! Having chimichurri on hand in the refrigerator means you can just slap a piece of something on the grill or in the broiler and dinner is ready.

Flank Steak with Zucchini and Yellow Squash "Pappardelle"

4 SERVINGS

> Salt
> 6 garlic cloves, chopped
> 6 tablespoons extra-virgin olive oil (EVOO), divided
> 2 tablespoons fresh thyme leaves, chopped
> 2 pounds flank steak
> Freshly ground black pepper
> 2 medium zucchini
> 2 medium yellow squash
> 1 teaspoon crushed hot red pepper flakes
> Zest and juice of 1 lemon
> 1/2 cup chicken stock or broth
> 2 tablespoons butter
> A handful fresh flat-leaf parsley, chopped
> 3/4 cup grated Parmigiano-Reggiano

Preheat a charcoal grill, grill pan, or large skillet (if using a large skillet for the steak, you might have to cut the steak in half to make it fit in the pan).

For the zucchini and yellow squash "pappardelle," in a large skillet bring 1 inch of salted water to a boil. Cover the skillet with a lid or a piece of foil so it comes to a boil quickly.

In a large shallow dish, combine half of the garlic, 3 tablespoons of the EVOO, and the thyme. Add the flank steak and coat completely in the mixture, allowing it to marinate for 5 to 10 minutes, depending on how much of a rush you are in. Season the flank steak with salt and pepper, place on the hot grill, and cook for 5 to 6 minutes per side. Remove from the grill and let rest for 5 minutes. While the steak is cooking, prepare the squash pappardelle.

Trim the ends off the zucchini and yellow squash, then slice lengthwise into ⅛-inch-thick slices. Assemble the long slices into a few stacks and then cut in half lengthwise to create the pappardelle, that is, large, wide ribbon shapes. Add the squash to the boiling water, cook for 1 minute, drain in a colander, and run cold water over them to stop the cooking. Transfer the squash ribbons to a clean kitchen towel and pat dry. Set aside.

Return the skillet to the stove and heat the remaining 3 tablespoons of EVOO over medium-high heat. Add the remaining garlic and the red pepper flakes and cook for 1 minute, or until the garlic starts to turn slightly brown. Be careful not to burn the garlic, but if you do, it will only take a minute or two to start over. Add the cooled dry squash pappardelle to the garlic and red pepper flakes and season with salt and pepper. Toss to combine and then add the lemon juice and chicken stock and continue to cook for 2 minutes, frequently and gently tossing but trying not to break up the squash pappardelle. Turn off the heat and add the butter, parsley, grated cheese, and lemon zest. Gently toss to melt the butter.

Thinly slice the flank steak on an angle and against the grain. Serve with the hot squash pappardelle.

TIDBIT

Pappardelle is a wide ribbon-shaped pasta, but in this recipe it is the shape of the zucchini and yellow squash.

London Broil and
String Beans Aglio e Olio

4 SERVINGS

- 2 pounds boneless shoulder steak
- 3 tablespoons Worcestershire sauce
- ¼ cup extra-virgin olive oil (EVOO) (4 times around the pan), plus some for drizzling
  Salt and freshly ground black pepper
- 2 pounds string beans, stems and strings trimmed
- 1 2-ounce tin anchovy fillets
- 6 to 8 large garlic cloves, crushed and minced
- 1 teaspoon crushed hot red pepper flakes
- ¼ cup finely chopped fresh flat-leaf parsley (a couple of handfuls)

Preheat a broiler on high and set the rack closest to the flame.

Fill a large skillet with 1 inch of water and bring to a boil for the beans.

Coat the steak with the Worcestershire sauce, drizzle EVOO on it, and season with salt and pepper. Put the steak on a broiler pan, situate the pan on the rack closest to the flame, and broil for 6 minutes per side. Remove from the broiler and allow the meat to rest for 5 minutes tented under aluminum foil.

While the steak is cooking, add a large pinch of salt to the boiling water, add the string beans, and cook for 2 to 3 minutes. Drain the string beans in a colander and run cold water over them to stop the cooking process. Dry out the skillet and place back on the burner over medium-low heat. Add about ¼ cup EVOO. Add the anchovies, garlic, and hot red pepper flakes to the oil. Break up the anchovies with a wooden spoon until they melt away into the oil and garlic mixture, about 2 minutes. Add the cold beans to the oil, toss to coat, and cook for 1 minute, or until the beans are heated through. Season beans with a little salt, to taste.

Slice the rested steak very thin, against the grain and on a slight angle. Serve the sliced meat alongside the string beans con aglio e olio.

CONFESSION

My go-to pasta dish has always been spaghetti con aglio e olio—that is, spaghetti with garlic and oil (and anchovies). It is cheap and easy to make. Since I've cut down on carbs, I am still eating pastas but now I go heavier on the veggies or meats I mix with it and easy on the pasta itself (see chapter 7). But for aglio e olio pasta, this concept does not apply. String beans aglio e olio help to satisfy my itch.

The trick to great London broil is a sharp knife. How tender it is really depends on how thin you can slice it. It's that simple.

Spinach-Stuffed Steaks with Sautéed Crimini Mushrooms

4 SERVINGS

- 1 package (10 ounces) chopped frozen spinach
- 4 tablespoons extra-virgin olive oil (EVOO)
- 3 garlic cloves, chopped
- ½ small yellow onion, chopped
- ½ small red bell pepper, ¼ chopped and ¼ cut into thin strips for garnish
- 2 ounces prosciutto di Parma, chopped
- ½ cup grated Parmigiano-Reggiano
  Freshly ground black pepper
- 2 pounds eye round roast, strings cut off
  Coarse salt
  Large plastic food storage bag

SAUTÉED CRIMINI MUSHROOMS

- 1 tablespoon extra-virgin olive oil (EVOO)
- 2 tablespoons butter
- 1½ pounds crimini mushrooms, brushed clean with damp towel
  Salt and freshly ground black pepper
- 3 tablespoons fresh thyme, chopped
- 1 pint grape tomatoes
- ½ cup dry red wine
- 2 tablespoons chopped fresh flat-leaf parsley

Defrost the spinach in the microwave, then wrap in a clean kitchen towel and twist to wring dry.

Heat a large skillet over medium-high heat. Add 2 tablespoons of the EVOO (twice around the pan), then the garlic, onion, and chopped bell pepper, and cook for 1 minute. Add the spinach and stir to incorporate it. Add the prosciutto and incorporate it. Add the cheese and black pepper and stir. Remove the stuffing from the heat and cool to handle.

To create a cavity for the stuffing, use a long, sharp knife, such as a boning knife, and cut into each end of the meat. Turn the knife to create a 2-inch hole through the center of meat, meeting the incisions at the middle of the roast. Twist the handle of a wooden spoon into the hole to loosen and widen the cavity, making the hole even for its entire length. Season the roast with the coarse salt.

Put the stuffing into a plastic food storage bag and cut a 1-inch hole in one bottom corner. Gather the bag, like a pastry bag, forcing the stuffing to that side. Stand the roast on its end and fill half the roast with stuffing. Turn on opposite end and finish filling the cavity by piping in the stuffing. You might need to push it along with your fingers to make sure it goes all the way through.

Preheat a large nonstick skillet over medium-high heat. Cut the roast into eight 1-inch-thick slices. Add the remaining 2 tablespoons of EVOO to the pan (2 turns of the pan). Add the meat and cook for 2 minutes, flip, cook 2 minutes more, then reduce heat to medium low and cook for 4 minutes more. Prepare the mushrooms while the meat cooks.

Heat a second large skillet over medium-high heat. Add the EVOO and butter. When the butter melts into the EVOO, add the mushrooms. Brown the mushrooms for 5 minutes, then season with salt, pepper, and thyme. Add the tomatoes and cook for 2 to 3 minutes more, until the tomatoes start to burst, then add the red wine and deglaze the pan. Finish with the parsley and turn off the heat.

Transfer 2 pieces of stuffed steak onto each of 4 dinner plates and garnish with the thinly sliced red bell pepper. Serve with a few spoonfuls of mushrooms alongside the steak.

Horseradish and Watercress-Stuffed Eye Round Roast with Mushroom and Bacon Ragout

4 SERVINGS

- 6 tablespoons extra-virgin olive oil (EVOO), divided
- 5 garlic cloves, chopped
- 1 small onion, chopped
- 1 bunch watercress, coarsely chopped
- 1¼ cups chicken stock or broth
- 2 tablespoons prepared grated horseradish
  Salt and freshly ground black pepper
- ¼ cup Italian bread crumbs (eyeball it)
- ⅓ to ½ cup grated Parmigiano-Reggiano (eyeball it)
- 2 pounds eye round roast, strings cut off
  Resealable plastic bag
- 4 slices bacon, chopped
- 3 pounds mixed mushrooms, such as portobello, shiitake, crimini, or oyster, brushed cleaned of dirt, trimmed of woody stems, and sliced
- 3 tablespoons fresh thyme leaves, chopped
- 3 tablespoons butter
  A handful of fresh flat-leaf parsley, chopped

Place a large skillet on the stove over medium-high heat with 2 tablespoons of the EVOO. Add three quarters of the chopped garlic, half of the onion, and the watercress and cook for 1 minute. Add ¼ cup of the chicken stock, the horseradish, salt, and pepper. Cook until there is only about 1 tablespoon left of the chicken stock, 2 to 3 minutes. Turn the heat off and add the bread crumbs and Parmigiano. Stir to combine and let the stuffing cool while you prepare the roast.

To create the cavity for the stuffing, use a long, sharp knife, such as a boning knife, and cut into each end of the roast. Turn the knife to create a 2-inch hole all the way through the center of the meat. Twist the handle of a wooden spoon into the cavity to make sure it is even.

Put the cooled filling in a resealable plastic bag and snip a $\frac{1}{2}$- to 1-inch hole in a corner of the bag. Stuff the snipped end of the bag about 1 to 2 inches into the cavity. Pipe the filling into the cavity. You might need to push it along with your fingers or the wooden spoon, to make sure that it goes all the way through. If you have any doubts, flip the meat over and pipe the filling from that end too.

Thoroughly wipe out the stuffing skillet and preheat it over medium-high heat with 2 tablespoons of the EVOO. Cut the roast into 8 even slices, being careful to keep the stuffing in each slice. Season the steaks with salt and pepper and sear in the hot skillet for 2 minutes on first side. Flip the steaks, sear for an additional 2 minutes, then lower the heat to medium low and cook until done, about 4 minutes more. Remove the meat from the skillet and allow it to rest for a few minutes before serving.

While the meat is cooking, start the mushrooms by heating a large skillet with the remaining 2 tablespoons of EVOO over medium-high heat. Add the chopped bacon and cook until crisp, about 3 minutes. Remove the crispy bacon to a plate lined with a paper towel and reserve. To the bacon skillet, add the mushrooms in an even layer covering the entire surface space of the skillet. Cook the mushrooms without stirring them for about 2 minutes. Stir them thoroughly, then let them set again for another 2 minutes. Add the remaining half of the onion, the remaining chopped garlic, the thyme, salt, and pepper. Stir to combine and continue to cook for 2 minutes. Add the remaining 1 cup of chicken stock and continue to cook until only $\frac{1}{2}$ cup of liquid remains in the pan, another couple of minutes. Remove the skillet from the heat, add the butter, and stir until melted. Finish the ragout with the chopped parsley and reserved bacon.

To serve, distribute the mushroom ragout among 4 dinner plates and top the ragout with 2 slices of stuffed eye round roast.

Saucy Buttered, Smothered Steaks with Spinach Gratin

4 SERVINGS

- 4 tablespoons extra-virgin olive oil (EVOO)
- 1 large Spanish onion, finely chopped
- 3 garlic cloves, chopped
- ¼ teaspoon grated or ground nutmeg
  Salt and freshly ground black pepper
- 2 10-ounce boxes frozen spinach, defrosted, squeezed dry of excess liquid
- ¾ cup chicken stock or broth
- 4 ounces plain cream cheese
- 1 cup (4 to 6 ounces) shredded Swiss cheese
- 2 tablespoons plain bread crumbs (optional)
- 3 tablespoons Worcestershire sauce (eyeball it)
- 1 tablespoon hot sauce, such as Tabasco (eyeball it)
- 8 ounces (1 stick) unsalted butter, softened
- 4 10-ounce sirloin strip steaks, 1 inch thick

Preheat the oven to 450°F.

For the spinach gratin, heat a medium skillet with 2 tablespoons of the EVOO over medium-high heat. Add the onion, garlic, nutmeg, salt, and pepper and cook for 2 minutes. Remove and reserve in a small mixing bowl 3 tablespoons of the cooked onion mixture to use in your saucy butter. To the remaining onion in the skillet, add the squeezed spinach, stirring to distribute the onion in the spinach. Next, add the chicken stock and continue to cook for 2 minutes. Add the cream cheese, stirring to distribute. Transfer the mixture to a small baking dish. Mix the shredded Swiss cheese with the plain bread crumbs. Top the spinach with the Swiss cheese mixture and transfer to the oven for 10 to 12 minutes, or until the top is golden brown.

For the saucy butter, add the Worcestershire sauce, hot sauce, salt, and pepper to the reserved onion mixture. Mix to combine, then add the soft butter. Mix to combine again and reserve in the refrigerator.

For the steaks, heat a large skillet over medium-high heat with the remaining 2 tablespoons of EVOO. Liberally season both sides of the steaks with salt and pepper. Add the steaks to the pan and cook for 5 to 6 minutes on each side. Remove from heat to a platter and top each steak with a rounded tablespoon of saucy butter. Allow the meat to rest and the butter to melt for 3 to 5 minutes. Serve steaks with the spinach gratin.

TIDBIT

Leftover butter can be frozen, well wrapped, for up to 6 months. Try it on not only beef but also on chicken, pork, or turkey.

Black Pepper Steaks with a Creamy Pan Sauce and Caramelized Zucchini

4 SERVINGS

$\frac{1}{2}$ cup extra-virgin olive oil (EVOO)

    Salt

4 small to medium T-bone steaks, no more than $1\frac{1}{2}$ inches thick

4 tablespoons freshly ground black pepper

2 large zucchini, cut into thin disks

3 garlic cloves, chopped

1 large Spanish onion, thinly sliced

2 plum tomatoes, cut in half lengthwise, seeds scraped out, then cut into thin strips

2 handfuls fresh flat-leaf parsley, chopped

1 tablespoon dry mustard powder or 2 tablespoons Dijon mustard

2 tablespoons thyme leaves (4 or 5 sprigs), chopped

1 cup chicken stock or broth

$\frac{1}{2}$ to $\frac{3}{4}$ cup heavy cream

For the steaks, preheat 2 skillets each with 2 tablespoons EVOO over medium-high heat. Season both sides of the steaks with salt. Press about $\frac{1}{2}$ tablespoon of freshly ground black pepper evenly on each side of the steaks. Add 2 seasoned steaks to each hot skillet and cook the steaks for 6 to 7 minutes on each side for medium doneness. If you have a huge skillet—14 inches—you can fit them all in one pan.

While the steaks are cooking, start the caramelized zucchini. Preheat a large skillet with 2 tablespoons of the EVOO over medium-high heat. Add the sliced zucchini, distributing it evenly over the entire surface of the skillet, and cook without stirring for 2 minutes. By not stirring the zucchini once you have it settled in the skillet, you will ensure that it will brown. Add the garlic, half of the sliced onion, and salt, and now you can stir it up to distribute the flavors. Cook for 5 minutes, tossing it occasionally. Add the tomatoes and half of the chopped parsley; continue to cook for 1 to 2 minutes, or until the tomatoes are heated through.

Remove the steaks from the skillet to a platter and tent with foil to rest while you make the sauce. With a rubber spatula, remove the excess pepper from the skillets, being sure to remove any burned bits but leaving the brown bits in the pan. Scrape all the drippings that remain into one skillet. Return the skillet with all the drippings to the heat and add the remaining 2 tablespoons of EVOO. Add the remaining sliced onion, the mustard, and thyme, and cook for 1 to 2 minutes, stirring frequently. Add the chicken stock and heavy cream, raise the heat to high, and cook for 3 minutes, or until the sauce is slightly thickened. Taste the sauce for seasoning, and then finish the sauce with the remaining chopped parsley.

To serve, top each steak with some of the sauce and serve alongside the caramelized zucchini.

TIDBIT

Zucchini is one of those vegetables that you love because it is inexpensive, fast, and easy to prepare. The thing is, it really doesn't have a great big flavor all on its own. By caramelizing it, you intensify the zucchini flavor.

East Coast Surf n' Turf: Rocket-Style Clams Casino and New York Strip Steaks with Roquefort-Watercress Salad

4 SERVINGS

- 4 tablespoons extra-virgin olive oil (EVOO)
- 4 12-ounce New York strip steaks, 1 inch thick
  - Salt and freshly ground black pepper
  - Rock salt or pickling salt (available on spice aisle in boxes)
- 24 cherrystone clams (buy them scrubbed, split them, and loosen clam)
- 8 ounces (1 stick) butter, softened
- 2 garlic cloves, finely chopped
- ½ bunch arugula (AKA rocket lettuce), washed and finely chopped by hand or in the food processor
  - Several drops of hot sauce (2 teaspoons)
- 4 slices center-cut bacon (lean and thin), cut into 24 1-inch pieces
- 3 ounces Roquefort cheese, crumbled
- ¼ small red onion, thinly sliced
- 3 tablespoons white wine vinegar
- 2 bunches watercress, trimmed of thick stems and torn into bite-size pieces

Preheat the oven to 500°F.

For the steaks, heat a large nonstick skillet over high heat or use 2 pans if necessary. Add 1 tablespoon of the EVOO to the pan. Season the steaks with salt and pepper. Place the steaks in the skillet and sear for 2 minutes on each side. Reduce heat to medium and cook the steaks 6 minutes longer for medium rare, 8 for medium to medium well. Remove the steaks to a warm plate to rest for 5 minutes. While the steaks are cooking, start the clams.

Pour rock salt into a shallow baking pan or dish. Set the clams upright into the salt. The salt will steady them. Mix the butter with the garlic, arugula, and hot sauce. Dab each clam with 1 teaspoon of the mixture and top with a piece of bacon. Bake for 7 to 8 minutes, until the bacon is crisp and the butter is brown and bubbling. Once the clams are cooking away in the oven, start the salad for the steaks.

In a bowl, combine the Roquefort, red onion, white wine vinegar, the remaining 3 tablespoons of EVOO, and salt and pepper. With a fork, mash up the cheese slightly, then give the mixture a little whisking. Add the watercress and toss to coat.

Have the rocket clams casino as an appetizer or serve alongside the New York strip steaks and the Roquefort-watercress salad.

Mediterranean Mixed Grill

4 SERVINGS

    Extra-virgin olive oil (EVOO), for drizzling
2   plum tomatoes, cut in half lengthwise
1   medium red onion, peeled and cut into 4 thick disks
1   small head fennel, cut in half through the root, each half cut into
    4 pieces held together by the root
1   yellow bell pepper, cored, seeded, and quartered
1   head radicchio, quartered
    Salt and freshly ground black pepper
    Balsamic vinegar, for drizzling
1   pound sweet Italian sausages
1   pound hot Italian sausages
1   pound raw large shrimp, peeled and deveined
2   garlic cloves, chopped
1   teaspoon crushed hot red pepper flakes
    A handful of fresh flat-leaf parsley, chopped
1   cup (20 leaves) fresh basil leaves, chopped
1   lemon

continued ....➤

The directions in this recipe are organized for an indoor grill pan. If you are using an outdoor grill, everything can go on the grill at one time.

Preheat a grill pan over high heat.

Drizzle EVOO liberally over the tomatoes, onion, fennel, bell pepper, and radicchio and season the vegetables with salt and pepper. Place on the grill and cook on each side for 3 minutes or until the vegetables are well marked and slightly tender but still have a little crunchy freshness to them. Remove from the grill and arrange on a large platter. Drizzle the vegetables with a little balsamic vinegar and cover with aluminum foil to keep warm.

Place the sausages on the grill and cook, turning occasionally, for 8 to 10 minutes, or until cooked through.

While the sausages are cooking, in a bowl combine the shrimp with 2 tablespoons of EVOO, the garlic, red pepper flakes, salt, and pepper. Once there is room on the grill, add the shrimp and cook on each side for 2 to 3 minutes. Add the cooked sausages and shrimp to the platter with the veggies. Sprinkle with the parsley and basil and squeeze the juice of 1 lemon over everything.

Veal Chops with Puttanesca Sauce and Alfredo Spaghetti Squash

4 SERVINGS

- 1 1-pound spaghetti squash, halved lengthwise and seeded
- 5 tablespoons extra-virgin olive oil (EVOO)
- 1 tin (2 ounces) anchovy fillets
- 6 to 8 large garlic cloves, crushed and chopped
- 1 teaspoon crushed hot red pepper flakes
  - A handful of pitted oil-cured olives, chopped
- 2 tablespoons capers, drained
- 1 can (14 ounces) diced tomatoes
- 4 bone-in rib veal chops, 1 to 1½ inches thick
  - Salt and freshly ground black pepper
- ½ cup grated Parmigiano-Reggiano
- 2 tablespoons butter
- ¼ cup finely chopped fresh flat-leaf parsley (a couple handfuls)

To a microwave-safe dish add ¼ inch of water. Place the spaghetti squash in the dish cut side down. Cover the dish tightly with plastic wrap. With a small knife puncture a few holes in the plastic so that the steam has a way to escape. Place the squash in the microwave on High power for 17 minutes.

Heat a medium skillet over medium-high heat with 3 tablespoons of the EVOO. Add the anchovies, garlic, and red pepper flakes. With a wooden spoon, mash the anchovies into the oil as it heats. The anchovies will begin to melt about after 1 to 2 minutes and they will develop a nutty flavor. Add the olives, capers, and tomatoes and bring it up to a simmer. Reduce the heat to medium low and simmer until ready to serve.

Heat a large skillet over medium-high heat with the remaining 2 tablespoons of EVOO. Liberally season the veal chops with salt

continued ....>

and pepper. Once the pan is screaming hot and you see the first wafts of smoke rising, add the chops to the hot skillet and cook on the first side for 5 minutes. Resist the temptation to move the chops around in the pan; you want a nice brown crust on them and messing with them won't help you get there. Before flipping the chops, reduce the heat to medium; flip and cook them on the second side for 8 to 10 minutes, or until desired doneness. Remove the chops from the pan and let them rest, covered with a foil tent for about 5 minutes.

Remove the spaghetti squash from the microwave very carefully—it is piping hot. Using a fork, scrape the "spaghetti" from the squash shell and place in a bowl. Toss the "spaghetti" with the Parmigiano-Reggiano, butter, parsley, salt, and pepper. Toss to coat.

Serve each chop with some of the puttanesca sauce on top and a portion of the "spaghetti Alfredo" alongside.

Veal Chops with Balsamic Pan Sauce and Spinach Salad with Pecans, Pears, and Gorgonzola

4 SERVINGS

- 1/2 cup pecan halves
- 5 tablespoons extra-virgin olive oil (EVOO)
- 4 bone-in rib veal chops, 1 1/2 inches thick
  Salt and freshly ground black pepper
- 7 to 8 fresh sage leaves, chopped
- 1/2 small yellow onion, chopped
- 2 garlic cloves, chopped
- 3 tablespoons balsamic vinegar (eyeball it)
- 1/2 cup chicken stock or broth

1 lemon

1 **pear**, your favorite variety, quartered, cored, and thinly sliced

1 sack of **baby spinach** (about 6 cups)

¼ pound crumbled **Gorgonzola cheese**, or Maytag Blue

2 tablespoons cold **butter**

Preheat the oven to 350°F.

Place the pecans on a baking sheet and toast in the oven for 8 to 10 minutes, or until they smell toasty and they are golden brown. Remove the nuts from the oven and cool them completely.

Heat a large skillet over medium-high heat with 2 tablespoons of the EVOO (twice around the pan). Liberally season the veal chops with salt, pepper, and sage. Once the skillet is screaming hot and you see the first wafts of smoke rising, add the chops and cook on the first side for 5 minutes. Resist the temptation to move the chops around in the pan; you want a nice brown crust on them and messing with them won't help you get there. Before flipping the chops, reduce the heat to medium; flip and cook them on the second side for 8 to 10 minutes, or until desired doneness. Remove the chops from the pan and let them rest under a foil tent for about 5 minutes.

While the chops are resting, make the sauce. To the same skillet, add a drizzle more EVOO, the onion, and garlic and cook for 1 minute. Add the balsamic vinegar and chicken stock and simmer for 2 to 3 minutes.

While the sauce is simmering, prepare the salad. In a salad bowl, combine the juice of 1 lemon with about 3 tablespoons of EVOO and a little salt and pepper. Add the sliced pear and toss to coat. Add the spinach, reserved toasted pecans, and crumbled Gorgonzola or Maytag Blue cheese. Toss to combine and coat.

Turn the heat off the balsamic pan sauce, add the cold butter, and swirl until completely melted. Serve each chop with a little balsamic pan sauce and a serving of the spinach salad.

Stuffed Veal Rolls with Pan-Roasted Garlic and Dressed-Up Mixed Greens

4 SERVINGS

- 6 garlic cloves, 4 crushed, 2 chopped
  Extra-virgin olive oil (EVOO), for liberal drizzling
- 2 hard-boiled eggs, chopped (see page 90)
- 1/2 cup fresh flat-leaf parsley, chopped
  Salt and freshly ground black pepper
- 8 pieces (1 1/2 to 1 1/3 pounds) veal shoulder scallopini
- 8 slices prosciutto di Parma
- 1/3 pound Italian fontina, sliced
  Toothpicks
- 3 tablespoons butter
- 1 tablespoon tomato paste
- 2 tablespoons fresh thyme, chopped
- 1/2 medium yellow onion, chopped
- 3/4 cup chicken stock or broth
- 1 heaping tablespoon Dijon mustard
- 3 tablespoons white wine vinegar
- 1 sack mixed greens (about 6 cups)

In a small saucepot combine the 4 crushed cloves of garlic with enough EVOO to cover them halfway, about 1/2 cup. Place the pot over the lowest possible heat setting of your cooktop. Gently cook the garlic for 10 minutes, frequently turning it in the oil to ensure even browning. Once the garlic is golden brown all over, turn the heat off and allow it to cool in the EVOO.

While the garlic is roasting, prepare the stuffed veal rolls. Combine the chopped hard-boiled eggs, the chopped parsley, and 2 crushed cloves of garlic in a bowl and season with a little salt and pepper. Taste and adjust the seasoning. This is your last chance to make sure the filling is up to par. Reserve the filling.

Lay the 8 pieces of scallopini out on the cutting board without overlapping any of the pieces. Season them with a little salt and pepper. Lay 1 slice of prosciutto on top of each scallopini. If necessary, fold the prosciutto so that it fits the veal without overhang. Add a thin slice of fontina cheese on top of the prosciutto. Place about 1 tablespoon of the egg-parsley mixture on the lower half of each scallopini. Starting at the point closest to you, roll each portion away from you into a cigar shape. Secure each veal roll with one or two toothpicks.

Heat a large skillet on high heat with 2 tablespoons of the EVOO and 2 tablespoons of the butter. Once the pan is hot and the butter is no longer foaming, add the 8 veal rolls. Brown on all sides, 3 to 4 minutes. Move the veal rolls over a little, clearing a spot in the skillet to add the remaining chopped garlic, the tomato paste, thyme, and onion. Continue to cook for 1 minute. Add the chicken stock and continue to cook for 3 to 4 minutes.

While the stuffed veal rolls are cooking, finish preparing the pan-roasted garlic dressing. In a blender combine the Dijon mustard and the white wine vinegar. Fish the golden brown garlic cloves from the oil and add to the blender. Blend on high for about 30 seconds. While the motor is still running, in a very slow and steady stream, add 3 to 4 tablespoons of the garlic cooking oil. Save the leftover garlic oil in the refrigerator. It will coagulate, but it will melt back down after a few minutes at room temp. The garlic oil is great for anything from marinades to sautéing greens.

Dress the mixed greens with the roasted garlic dressing. To finish the stuffed veal rolls, turn the heat off and remove the veal rolls from the skillet to a platter. Finish the sauce with 1 tablespoon of butter, swirling it into the sauce until it is completely melted. Remove the toothpicks from the veal and pour the sauce over the veal. Serve with the salad.

Veal Chops with Raw Sauce

4 SERVINGS

  4 vine-ripe tomatoes, cut into 8 wedges, each wedge cut in half
 10 fresh basil leaves, torn
     A handful of fresh flat-leaf parsley, coarsely chopped
  1 small red onion, thinly sliced
     Salt and freshly ground black pepper
  3 tablespoons balsamic vinegar
 ¼ cup extra-virgin olive oil (EVOO)
  4 bone-in rib veal chops, 1 to 1½ inches thick
  1 pound fresh spinach, trimmed of thick stems and washed
 ½ cup pitted kalamata olives, coarsely chopped

In a bowl combine the tomatoes, basil, parsley, onion, salt, pepper, balsamic vinegar, and about 2 tablespoons of the EVOO. Allow the tomatoes to sit for 10 minutes so that the salt will leach out the juice of the tomatoes.

Heat a large skillet over medium-high heat with the remaining 2 tablespoons of EVOO (twice around the pan). Liberally season the veal chops with salt and pepper. Once the skillet is screaming hot and you see the first wafts of smoke rising, add the chops to the hot skillet and cook on the first side for 5 minutes. Resist the temptation to move the chops around in the pan; you want a nice brown crust on them and messing with them won't help you get there. Before flipping the chops, reduce the heat to medium; flip and cook them on the second side for 7 to 8 minutes, or until desired doneness. Remove the chops from the pan and allow to rest, tented with foil, for about 5 minutes.

Once the chops are cooked and rested, add the spinach and olives to the tomatoes and toss to coat. Serve the chops on top of some of the salad and spoon out some of the tomato balsamic juice from the bottom of the salad bowl to top each chop.

Turkey Cutlet Gyro Wraps

4 SERVINGS

- 3 tablespoons extra-virgin olive oil (EVOO)
- 2 tablespoons ground cumin (2 palmfuls)
- 1 tablespoon dried oregano (a palmful)
- 3 garlic cloves, chopped

  Juice of 1 lemon

  Salt and freshly ground black pepper
- 2 pounds turkey breast cutlets
- 1 cup whole-milk plain yogurt
- ¼ cup fresh dill, chopped
- 1 bunch scallions, white and green parts, finely chopped
- 1 small red onion, sliced
- 1 bunch (about 10 ounces) flat-leaf spinach, washed and coarsely chopped
- ½ English (seedless) cucumber (the one wrapped in plastic), diced into bite-size chunks
- 1 can (15 ounces) chickpeas, drained and well rinsed
- 1 cup crumbled feta cheese
- 2 heads Bibb or Boston lettuce, leaves separated, washed, and dried and left whole

Preheat an outdoor grill, an indoor grill pan, a tabletop grill, or a large nonstick skillet to medium-high heat.

In a shallow bowl large enough to accommodate all the turkey, combine the EVOO, cumin, oregano, garlic, the lemon juice, salt, and pepper. Add the turkey and coat completely in the seasoning mixture. Grill the cutlets, working in 2 batches if necessary, for 4 to 5 minutes on each side, or until cooked through.

While the cutlets are grilling, assemble the dressing and the rest of the ingredients. For the dressing, in a small bowl combine the yogurt, dill, and scallions, and set aside.

In a salad bowl combine the red onion, spinach, cucumber, chickpeas, and feta cheese. Toss to combine.

continued ....➤

When the turkey is finished cooking, remove from the grill and cut into thin strips. Add the strips of turkey to the bowl with the spinach while the turkey is still hot. Toss the turkey strips and spinach together; the spinach will wilt a bit. Dress with the yogurt dressing and toss to coat completely.

Fill each whole lettuce cup with some of the turkey-spinach mixture, rolling the lettuce around the filling. Eat and enjoy.

Turkey Cutlets with No-Bread Stuffing and Pan Gravy, Smashed Garlic-and-Herb Cauliflower

4 SERVINGS

1 large head cauliflower
3 cups chicken stock or broth
3 tablespoons extra-virgin olive oil (EVOO)
5 tablespoons butter, cut into pieces
1 medium onion, chopped
3 celery ribs with greens, chopped
2 apples, any variety, cored and chopped
1 pound kale, coarsely chopped
Coarse salt and coarse black pepper
A healthy grating of nutmeg
8 pieces turkey breast cutlet
2 teaspoons poultry seasoning
2 tablespoons flour
1 tablespoon Worcestershire sauce (eyeball it)
1 (5-ounce) Boursin garlic and herb cheese

Remove the greens and the main core of the cauliflower with a small, sharp knife. You can leave the whole head otherwise intact. Pour 1 cup of the stock into a medium pot. Place the cauliflower head into the pot. Bring the liquid up to a boil and cover the pot. Reduce heat and simmer the cauliflower for 10 minutes, or until just tender all over. Remove the lid and allow the liquid to cook off and reduce, about 2 minutes. Cook the stuffing while the cauliflower is working.

Preheat a medium skillet over medium-high heat, then add 1 tablespoon of the EVOO and 3 tablespoons of the butter. When the butter melts into the oil, add the onion, celery, and apples and cook for 5 to 6 minutes. Add the kale and turn to wilt it into the vegetables and apples. Season the mixture with salt, pepper, and nutmeg to taste. Turn the pan to low and reserve.

Heat a large nonstick skillet over medium-high heat. Season the cutlets with poultry seasoning, salt, and pepper. Add the remaining 2 tablespoons of EVOO to the pan and as soon as you see a waft of smoke, add the cutlets and cook for 3 or 4 minutes on each side. Remove to a plate and tent with foil. Add the remaining 2 tablespoons of butter to the pan and melt it. Whisk in the flour and cook for 1 minute. Whisk in the remaining 2 cups of stock and the Worcestershire, and season the gravy with salt and pepper. Reduce and thicken for 2 to 3 minutes.

To finish off the cauliflower, mash with a potato masher. Add Boursin cheese, crumbling it up as it goes into the pot, then mash to combine and season the cauliflower with salt and pepper.

To serve, layer a cutlet with a big helping of no-bread stuffing, top with another cutlet, and pour a ladle of gravy down over top. Serve smashed cauliflower mounded up alongside.

Individual Turkey Meatloaf and Broccoli with Cheddar Cheese Sauce

4 SERVINGS

1⅓ pounds ground lean turkey (average weight of 1 package)

1 tablespoon grill seasoning (a palmful, such as McCormick's Montreal Steak Seasoning)

2 teaspoons poultry seasoning (⅔ palmful)

⅓ cup bottled barbecue sauce, any brand

1 small or ½ medium zucchini, diced fine

½ small red bell pepper, seeded, cored, and diced fine

3 scallions, finely chopped

¾ cup smoked almonds, such as Diamond brand, ground in food processor to bread-crumb consistency

1 egg yolk, beaten
Extra-virgin olive oil (EVOO), for drizzling

1 large head broccoli or 2 small heads

2 tablespoons butter

2 tablespoons flour

1 cup chicken stock or broth

1 cup milk

2½ cups (10 ounces) good-quality shredded Cheddar cheese

2 teaspoons Tabasco sauce
Salt

1 cup store-bought chipotle, tomato, or tomatillo salsa, any brand

Preheat the oven to 425°F.

Place the turkey in a medium mixing bowl and make a deep well in the center by punching the meat with your fist. Fill the well with the grill seasoning, poultry seasoning, barbecue sauce, chopped veggies, ground smoked almonds (clever sub for bread crumbs, I know, plus the smoked nuts rock with the BBQ sauce), and egg yolk. Mix the meatloaf ingredients together, then score the meat with your hand into 4 equal sections. Form 4 individual oval loaves, each 1½ inches thick. Arrange on a nonstick baking sheet and drizzle liberally with EVOO. Roast the meatloaves for 18 to 20 minutes. While they roast, work on the broccoli and Cheddar sauce.

Trim the very end off of the broccoli stems. With a peeler or a paring knife, remove the thick, fibrous outer layer of the broccoli stems all the way up to within an inch of where the broccoli shoots off into its florets. Cut the broccoli lengthwise into large spears.

Heat a small or medium saucepot over medium heat and add the butter. When the butter melts, whisk in the flour and cook for 1 minute. Whisk in the chicken stock, then the milk. Thicken for 2 minutes, then stir in the cheese and melt, 2 minutes. Season with the Tabasco and salt to taste, then turn the heat to low.

Bring a couple of cups of water to a boil in a deep skillet. Add salt and broccoli and cook the spears for about 5 minutes in simmering water, until tender but still green. Drain and return to the pan to remain warm.

Place a turkey meatloaf on a dinner plate. Garnish with a spoonful or two of salsa. Pile some broccoli spears alongside and top with a generous ladle of cheese sauce.

Greek Chicken Skewers with Fired-Up Cheese

4 SERVINGS

    Bamboo skewers, 8 inches or longer
1 English (seedless) cucumber (the one wrapped in plastic)
2 large garlic cloves, finely chopped
3 lemons
    Salt and freshly ground black pepper
1 cup whole-milk plain yogurt
1½ pounds chicken tenders (about 20 pieces)
1 tablespoon fresh oregano or marjoram, chopped, or ½ tablespoon dried
5 tablespoons extra-virgin olive oil (EVOO)
1 egg
¼ cup flour (relax, it's not that much)
    1-pound wedge of Kasseri cheese, ½ inch to 1 inch thick
1 tablespoon butter
2 ounces Ouzo or Grappa
    A handful of fresh flat-leaf parsley, chopped

Preheat a charcoal grill or grill pan on high. Submerge the skewers in warm water as this will help prevent them from burning up on the grill or grill pan.

With a box grater, grate the cucumber onto a clean kitchen towel. Wrap the kitchen towel around the grated cucumber and squeeze out the water. Place the squeezed, grated cucumber in a mixing bowl and add half of the chopped garlic, the juice of 1 lemon, a little salt, and a lot of freshly ground black pepper. Mix in the yogurt and reserve.

Combine the chicken tenders in a bowl with the juice of 1 lemon, the oregano or marjoram, the other half of the chopped garlic, about 2 tablespoons of the EVOO, salt, and pepper. Toss to coat the chicken completely. Thread the chicken onto skewers. Place on the grill for 3 minutes per side, or until cooked through.

Crack the egg into a shallow dish and thoroughly whisk. Dust the wedge of cheese in the flour and shake off the excess. Place the flour-coated cheese in the beaten egg and flip to coat completely. Place the cheese back into the flour, coating it on both sides lightly.

Preheat a large nonstick skillet over medium-high heat with the remaining 3 tablespoons of EVOO (3 times around the pan). Once you see the first waft of smoke rising from the pan, add the butter and swirl it in the pan to melt. Once melted, carefully add the coated cheese wedge, browning it on each side, 2 minutes per side. Remove the pan from the heat and add the Ouzo or Grappa, then replace the pan on the heat. Stand back and be careful: The pan will flame up. Once the flame extinguishes, squeeze the juice of the last lemon over the cheese and sprinkle with the parsley. Platter up the fired-up cheese and serve alongside the chicken skewers topped with a liberal dose of the cucumber-yogurt mixture.

Devilish Chicken and Cool Green Beans

4 SERVINGS

- 3 tablespoons extra-virgin olive oil (EVOO)
- 2 teaspoons paprika
- 1 teaspoon dry mustard or 1 tablespoon spicy mustard
  Salt and freshly ground black pepper
- 4 boneless, skinless chicken breasts, 6 to 8 ounces each
- 1 medium onion, thinly sliced
- 4 garlic cloves, chopped
- 1 red bell pepper, cored, seeded, quartered lengthwise, and sliced into thin strips
- 1 tablespoon tomato paste
- 1 teaspoon crushed hot red pepper flakes
- 1½ cups chicken stock or broth
- 1 to 1½ pounds green beans, stem end trimmed
- 10 fresh mint leaves, chopped
  A handful of fresh flat-leaf parsley, chopped
- 2 tablespoons cold butter

In a large skillet, heat 2 tablespoons of the EVOO (twice around the pan) over medium-high heat. Mix the paprika and mustard with some salt and pepper and season chicken breasts on both sides. Add the seasoned chicken to the skillet and brown on the first side for 3 minutes, flip, and then sear the second side, 2 minutes. Remove the chicken and reserve on a plate under a foil tent. To the pan, add the onion, garlic, bell pepper, tomato paste, and red pepper flakes. Cook the vegetables for 5 minutes, stirring frequently. Add 1 cup of the chicken stock to the vegetables and bring it to a simmer. Add the reserved chicken back to the pan and cook for 10 minutes more, turning the chicken over every now and then.

While the chicken is cooking, prepare the cool green beans. Heat a medium skillet with the remaining tablespoon of EVOO, then add the green beans, season with salt and pepper, and cook for 1 minute. Add the remaining ½ cup of chicken stock and continue to cook for 3 to 4 minutes, or until the green beans are tender. Add the mint and half of the parsley.

Remove the chicken from the skillet to a platter. To finish the sauce, turn the heat off and add the remaining parsley and butter, stirring to melt the butter. Pour the sauce over the chicken. Serve both the chicken and green beans immediately.

Impossibly Good Chicken and Simple Mixed Greens Salad

4 SERVINGS

- 5 tablespoons extra-virgin olive oil (EVOO)
- 6 6-ounce boneless, skinless chicken breasts, each cut into 4 large chunks
  Salt and freshly ground black pepper
- 1 small yellow onion, thinly sliced
- 1 red bell pepper, cored, seeded, and cut into thin strips
- 4 garlic cloves, chopped
- 3 cups chicken stock or broth
- ¾ cup heavy cream
- ½ pint grape or small cherry tomatoes
- ½ cup pitted green olives, roughly chopped (optional)
- 1 tablespoon Dijon mustard
- 3 tablespoons red wine vinegar
- 1 sack of mixed greens (about 6 cups)
- 2 cups fresh basil (about 40 leaves), torn or chopped
- 2 handfuls fresh flat-leaf parsley, chopped

continued ....➤

Heat a large, deep skillet on medium high with 2 tablespoons of the EVOO. Add the chicken to the hot skillet when the oil begins to smoke, then season liberally with salt and pepper. Brown the chicken on both sides; you are looking for an amber color, about 7 minutes. Add the onion, bell pepper strips, and garlic to the pan and continue to cook for 2 minutes. Add the chicken stock and the cream, then bring the sauce up to a hard simmer. Simmer for about 4 to 5 minutes; the stock and cream should reduce and begin to thicken slightly. Add the tomatoes and olives next and continue to cook for 2 to 3 more minutes. While the chicken is simmering, put the salad together.

In a small bowl, combine the mustard and vinegar. In a slow, steady stream, whisk in the remaining 3 tablespoons of EVOO. Place the mixed greens in a salad bowl, toss together with the dressing, and season with salt and pepper. By all means, have a peek in the fridge for any other veggies for the salad—anything goes! When we're talking veggies, the more the merrier!

To finish the chicken, add all that basil and parsley, stirring to distribute. Give it a taste, checking to see if you need more salt and pepper. Serve immediately with the simple tossed salad. (It's impossibly good, right?)

TIDBIT

When browning large amounts of meat, use a pot or skillet that looks too big. Forcing too much food into too small a pan results in rubbery textures and uneven browning. If you don't have a big pan, then use two pans. Your recipe will have the same cooking time and the meats will all brown correctly, giving your completed dishes better flavor.

Prosciutto-Wrapped Endive and Radicchio with Balsamic-Fig Reduction

4 SERVINGS

- 2 heads Belgian endive, quartered lengthwise
- 2 small heads radicchio, quartered lengthwise
  Salt and freshly ground black pepper
- ¼ pound sliced prosciutto, slices cut in half on an angle across the center
  Extra-virgin olive oil (EVOO), for brushing
- 2 dried figs, finely chopped
- ½ cup balsamic vinegar

Preheat a grill pan over medium-high heat.

Season the endive and radicchio with salt and pepper. Wrap each quarter with a half slice of prosciutto. Brush the bundles with EVOO and grill for 7 to 8 minutes, turning occasionally, until the prosciutto is crispy and the greens are tender. Transfer to a platter.

Place the figs and vinegar in a pot and bring to a boil, then reduce the heat to a simmer. Reduce the vinegar down to a few tablespoons, until the fig pieces are soft and the vinegar is thick, 5 minutes. Drizzle back and forth over the grilled bundles.

Hazelnut-Crusted Chicken with Gorgonzola Sauce

4 SERVINGS

- 2 tablespoons flour (hey, there's no bread crumbs, get over the 2 tablespoons!)
- 1 teaspoon poultry seasoning
- 1 teaspoon garlic powder
- 2 large egg whites
- 1 cup chopped hazelnuts
- 4 6-ounce boneless, skinless chicken breasts
  Salt and freshly ground black pepper
- 2 tablespoons extra-virgin olive oil (EVOO)
- 1 cup whole milk
- ½ cup Gorgonzola cheese
- 2 tablespoons chopped fresh sage or 1 teaspoon dried sage, for garnish

Preheat the oven to 325°F.

Mix the flour, poultry seasoning, and garlic powder on a dish. Beat the egg whites in a shallow plate or bowl. Place the hazelnuts on a piece of wax paper or plastic spread on a cutting board or work surface.

Preheat a nonstick skillet with an oven-safe handle over medium to medium-high heat. Season the chicken with salt and pepper. Turn in flour to dust the breasts, then turn them in the egg whites, then press the breasts into the nuts on both sides. Wash hands. Add EVOO to the pan and add the chicken. Brown the nuts-crusted chicken for 2 minutes on each side, then transfer to the oven and finish cooking the chicken through, 8 to 10 minutes. While the chicken cooks, start the recipe for Prosciutto-Wrapped Endive and Radicchio, page 193.

Shortly before serving, warm the milk over medium heat in a small pot. Add the cheese and melt it into the milk. If using dried sage, stir it into the sauce. Simmer for 5 minutes.

To serve, place the chicken on plates and pour a couple of spoons of the Gorgonzola sauce over the center of each piece. Garnish with chopped fresh sage, if using.

Chicken au Gratin

4 SERVINGS

- 4 tablespoons extra-virgin olive oil (EVOO)
- 1 pound button mushrooms, stems discarded, cleaned
- 2 tablespoons fresh thyme leaves (3 to 4 sprigs), chopped
- 2 garlic cloves, chopped
- 4 6- to 8-ounce boneless, skinless chicken breasts, cut into bite-size pieces
  Salt and freshly ground black pepper
- 1½ cups frozen pearl onions, defrosted
- 3 cups chicken stock or broth
- ¾ cup heavy cream
- 1 cup frozen peas
  A handful of fresh flat-leaf parsley, chopped
  Zest and juice of 1 lemon
- ¼ cup plain bread crumbs
- ½ cup grated Parmigiano-Reggiano
- 2 tablespoons cold butter, cut into small pieces
- 6 cups mixed greens

Heat a large skillet over medium-high heat with 2 tablespoons of the EVOO (twice around the pan). Add the mushrooms and brown, about 4 minutes. Add the thyme, garlic, chicken, salt, and pepper. Cook for 3 minutes. Add the pearl onions and cook for 1 minute. Add the chicken stock and cream; cook for 5 minutes.

continued ....➤

Add the peas, parsley, and lemon zest. Toss to combine and cook for 1 minute while you make the topping.

In a bowl, combine the bread crumbs and Parmigiano cheese. Transfer the chicken mixture to a baking dish and evenly sprinkle the top with the bread-crumb–cheese mixture. Dot the topping with cold butter pieces. Place under the broiler and brown, 1 to 3 minutes. Serve with a simple mixed green salad tossed together with the lemon juice and the remaining 2 tablespoons of olive oil.

CONFESSION

Yes, I know it's shocking, the bread crumbs and all. Climb on down off the ceiling because you can borrow my rationalization: The way I see it, ¼ cup of bread crumbs, split among 4 people, is so little, it's like you aren't eating bread crumbs at all. (Or, at least that's what I say to myself.)

Grilled Citrus Chicken with Goat Cheese Salad

I'm on a never-ending search for different ways to prepare chicken, and I have one rule: Don't make it different by making it more complicated. This chicken dish is simple, delicious, *and* different. It's particularly great if you have company coming over. It will free you up so you can actually hang out, too!

4 SERVINGS

Zest and juice of 1 lime
Zest and juice of 1 orange
Zest and juice of 1 lemon
1 large garlic clove, chopped
6 tablespoons extra-virgin olive oil (EVOO)
Salt and freshly ground black pepper
4 6- to 8-ounce boneless, skinless chicken breasts
1 bunch watercress, washed and slightly torn into pieces
1 sack (about 6 ounces) of prewashed arugula
4 to 6 ounces fresh goat cheese, crumbled
½ cup sliced almonds, toasted

Heat a grill pan or nonstick skillet over medium-high heat.

Combine the zest of the lime, orange, and lemon in a bowl, then add the garlic and the juice of the orange. Whisk in 3 tablespoons of the EVOO. Season with salt and pepper. Turn the chicken in the mixture and let it hang out for 5 to 10 minutes. Grill or pan-fry it for 6 minutes on each side, or until cooked through. Remove from heat and let rest for 5 minutes while you prepare the salad.

For the salad dressing, combine the juice of the lime and lemon with salt and pepper. Whisk in the remaining 3 tablespoons of EVOO and reserve. In a large bowl combine the watercress, arugula, goat cheese, and toasted almonds. Toss with the dressing.

Slice the chicken on an angle and serve it atop a pile of the salad.

BBQ Drumsticks and Mustardy Mustard Greens

4 SERVINGS

- 12 chicken drumsticks
  Salt and freshly ground black pepper
- 2 tablespoons vegetable oil, plus some for drizzling
- 1 large sweet onion, such as Vidalia, chopped
- 6 garlic cloves, chopped
- 3 tablespoons chili powder
- 1 teaspoon ground cinnamon
- 3 tablespoons honey
- 4 tablespoons tomato paste
- ¾ cup yellow mustard
- ¾ cup cider vinegar
- 3 tablespoons Worcestershire sauce
- 1¼ to 1½ cups chicken stock or broth
- 4 slices bacon, chopped
- 6 to 8 cups chopped mustard greens (2 bundles), trimmed and chopped

Preheat a broiler to high and situate the rack 6 to 8 inches from heat source.

Place the drumsticks on a slotted broiler pan and season them liberally with salt and pepper. Drizzle the drumsticks with a little vegetable oil and place under the broiler for 6 minutes. Flip the drumsticks and place them back under the broiler for another 6 minutes. While the drumsticks are broiling, start the BBQ sauce.

Heat a small saucepan with 1 tablespoon vegetable oil over high heat. Add half of the onion, 2 of the chopped garlic cloves, salt, pepper, the chili powder, and cinnamon. Cook for 1 minute, stirring frequently. Add the honey, tomato paste, ½ cup of the yellow mustard, ½ cup of the cider vinegar, the Worcestershire sauce, and ¾ cup of the chicken stock. Bring the sauce up to a simmer; turn down the heat to medium and cook for 5 to 8 minutes, or until thickened.

While the sauce is working, heat a large skillet over medium-high heat with 1 tablespoon of vegetable oil (once around the pan). Add the chopped bacon and cook until crisp, about 3 minutes. Remove the bacon to a plate lined with a paper towel to drain. Raise the heat to high and add the remaining half of the onion and 4 chopped garlic cloves. Cook them together, stirring frequently, for 1 to 2 minutes. Add the chopped mustard greens, tossing to coat. Add the remaining ¼ cup mustard and ¼ cup cider vinegar. Stir to distribute. Season the greens with salt and pepper, and stir until the mustard greens begin to wilt, a minute or two. Add the remaining ½ cup chicken stock, bring it up to a simmer, and then lower the heat to medium. Cook the greens for 8 to 10 minutes, until tender and spicy but no longer bitter. If all the stock cooks away before they are done, add a little more as you go.

To finish off the drumsticks, remove them from the broiler and pour the BBQ sauce over them. Using tongs, coat the drumsticks completely in the sauce. Place the coated drumsticks back under the broiler and broil for 2 to 3 minutes. Flip and broil for another 2 to 3 minutes. Using a paring knife, have a peek inside the drumsticks to ensure that they are cooked through before serving.

Transfer the "mustardy" mustard greens to a platter and garnish with the reserved crispy bacon. Serve alongside the BBQ drumsticks.

CONFESSION

Any lifestyle-changing diet can be hard to stick to. I try to give myself the tools for success; in this case that means having ready-to-eat meaty items in the refrigerator. I tire of snacking on cold cuts and salami and need to switch it up and choose the double-duty route. The BBQ drumsticks are a great ready-to-go snack that can be munched while on the move.

Pecan-Crusted Chicken with Celeriac-Parsnip Smash and Lemon-Mustard Mixed Greens

If you prefer a smoother consistency, by all means, purée the cooked celeriac and parsnips in a food processor.

4 SERVINGS

- 2 medium parsnips, peeled and cut into 1-inch chunks
- 2 small bulbs celeriac, about 1½ pounds, completely trimmed and peeled (use a paring knife), cut into 1-inch chunks
  Salt
- ½ to ¾ cup heavy cream or half-and-half
- 2 tablespoons butter
  Freshly ground black pepper
- 2 cups pecan halves, ground in a food processor until finely chopped, like bread crumbs
- ½ teaspoon cayenne pepper
- 2 eggs, lightly beaten
- 2 pounds chicken tenders
- ½ cup vegetable oil (eyeball it)
  Juice of 1 lemon
- 2 teaspoons dry mustard or 1 rounded tablespoon Dijon mustard
- ⅓ cup extra-virgin olive oil (EVOO)
- 6 cups mixed greens

For the celeriac-parsnip smash, place the parsnips and celeriac in a saucepan and add enough water to cover. Add a little salt and bring to a boil over high heat; cook until tender, 8 to 10 minutes. Drain in a colander and then return to the pot. Smash the cooked root vegetables with a fork or potato masher to desired consistency. Add the cream and butter and season with salt and pepper to taste. While the smash is cooking, prepare the chicken.

In a shallow dish, combine the ground pecans and the cayenne pepper. In another shallow dish, place the lightly beaten eggs. Put the chicken tenders in the eggs, coating them completely. Draw them from the eggs, allowing the excess egg to drip off. Place the egg-coated chicken in the nut mixture and coat completely.

Heat a large skillet with the vegetable oil over medium heat. As soon as you see a little ripple in the oil, add the pecan-coated chicken. Cook on each side for 3 to 4 minutes. Remove the chicken to a plate lined with a paper towel and season with salt while still hot. While the chicken is cooking, prepare the salad.

In a small mixing bowl combine the lemon juice and mustard. Add a little salt and pepper and whisk in the EVOO. Add the mixed greens to a salad bowl and toss with the lemon-mustard dressing.

Slice the pecan-crusted chicken and fan out on top of a bed of the salad. Serve the smashed root vegetables alongside.

TIDBIT

Celeriac is not pretty, but it is very tasty. It's celery root, or "celery knob," and, yup, being related and all, it tastes like a cross between celery and parsley. It makes a great lower-carb alternative to potatoes.

Parmesan-Crusted Chicken Breasts with Pesto Sauce and Big-Mushroom–Veggie Sauté

4 SERVINGS

- 4 tablespoons extra-virgin olive oil (EVOO)
- 4 6-ounce boneless, skinless chicken breasts
  Salt and freshly ground black pepper
- 2 cups store-bought shredded domestic Parmesan cheese
- 3 portobello mushroom caps, gills scraped off with a spoon, thinly sliced
- 1/2 small Spanish onion, finely chopped
- 2 garlic cloves, chopped
- 1 bunch thin asparagus, ends trimmed and discarded, spears chopped into 2-inch lengths
- 3 tablespoons good-quality aged sherry vinegar, or red wine vinegar
- 3/4 cup chicken stock or broth
- 1/2 pint cherry tomatoes, whole if small, halved if large
  A handful of fresh flat-leaf parsley chopped
- 6 ounces good-quality store-bought pesto (from the dairy aisle)

Heat a large nonstick skillet over medium to medium-high heat with 2 tablespoons of the EVOO (twice around the pan). Season both sides of the chicken breasts with salt and pepper. Dump out the cheese onto a plate and press the chicken into the cheese, covering all the pieces in cheese on both sides. Add the chicken to the hot skillet, allowing it to cook a full 6 to 7 minutes—DO NOT MESS WITH THE BIRD! The Parmesan is browning and melting together to form an all-cheese, no-bread-crumb crust all over the chicken. After 7 minutes (or when the chicken budges easily), turn and cook the chicken 5 to 6 minutes more.

While the chicken is browning, heat another large skillet over high heat with the remaining 2 tablespoons of EVOO. Add the mushrooms and season with pepper. Brown the mushrooms for 3 minutes. Season the mushrooms with salt and add the onion and garlic. Cook for 2 minutes, stirring occasionally. Add the asparagus, tossing to combine. Add the sherry vinegar and continue to cook until the skillet is almost dry, about 1 minute. Add the chicken stock and cherry tomatoes and cook for 3 minutes, or until the asparagus is tender. Add the parsley, tossing to coat.

Top the chicken with a strip of pesto across each breast. Serve a pile of the big-mushroom–veggie sauté alongside each breast.

TIDBITS

Removing the gills from the mushrooms is only done for aesthetic reasons. The gills will blacken the other veggies as they cook together. If you don't mind that, then you can skip the scraping.

Holding off on seasoning the mushrooms with salt will help you get the mushrooms a nice, deep brown color. Salt brings out the water in the mushrooms, so while salting might help them soften faster it will slow their browning.

Grilled Eggplant and Capicola Parmigiana

No bread crumbs, plus it's not deep-fried! You could eat a mountain of this eggplant parm and not have to loosen your belt.

4 SERVINGS

- 1 cup extra-virgin olive oil (EVOO) (eyeball it)
- 4 garlic cloves, crushed
- 2 medium eggplant, ends cut off, sliced crosswise, ¾ inch thick
  Salt
- 1 teaspoon coarse black pepper
- 1 medium yellow onion, finely chopped
- 1 can (28 ounces) crushed tomatoes
- 1 teaspoon ground cumin (⅓ palmful)
- ¼ teaspoon ground cinnamon
  A handful of fresh flat-leaf parsley, finely chopped
- ½ pound deli-sliced capicola hot ham
- ½ cup grated Parmigiano-Reggiano
- 6 pieces sharp deli-sliced provolone
- 6 cups mixed greens, any variety
- 2 tablespoon red wine vinegar

Preheat the oven to 450°F.

Combine the EVOO and garlic in a small pot over medium-low heat. When the garlic simmers, reduce heat to low.

Brush the eggplant on both sides with the garlic-infused EVOO and arrange on a baking sheet. Season the eggplant with salt and the pepper and place in the oven to roast. Use a double-folded piece of foil to make a second baking surface if the eggplant won't fit on your baking sheet. Roast the eggplant for 15 to 18 minutes, turning once, until browned at the edges, lightly golden, and just tender to the touch. While it roasts, prepare the sauce.

From the remaining EVOO, fish out the garlic and chop it up. Heat a small to medium pot over medium heat. Add about 2 tablespoons of the garlic-infused EVOO and the chopped garlic. Add the onion and cook for 10 minutes, stirring frequently. Add the tomatoes, salt, pepper, cumin, and cinnamon and heat through. Simmer for 5 minutes. Stir in half of the parsley. Remove the eggplant from the oven and switch the broiler on high.

To make your casserole, ladle a little of the tomato sauce in the bottom of a casserole and add a layer of eggplant, then a layer of capicola, then the remaining eggplant, remaining sauce, Parmigiano, provolone, and the remaining parsley. Broil until the cheese is brown and bubbly, about 3 minutes.

Place the salad greens in a bowl and toss with the vinegar, then 3 tablespoons of EVOO (use remaining garlic oil if you still have some left), and season the salad with salt and pepper to taste.

Serve the eggplant parm alongside a little green salad.

HEADS-UP!

I am already preaching moderation when it comes to carbs just in my use of tomato anything, as tomatoes are fruits and fruits have some natural carbs. I feel I can get away with a lower-carb life by not denying myself tomatoes, especially because of all of their other health benefits, touted in the health news of late. But, be careful when purchasing tomatoes of any kind in a can: Check to make sure the product is sugar free. More foods than any of us would care to know about, and especially tomatoes, are spiked with unnatural and additional sweeteners and sugars.

Grilled Chicken Parmigiana

No bread crumbs and it's not fried. Eat two portions. Life is good.

4 SERVINGS

2 pounds thin chicken breast cutlets

Salt and freshly ground black pepper

Extra-virgin olive oil (EVOO), for drizzling, plus 5 tablespoons

3 to 4 garlic cloves, chopped

1 teaspoon crushed hot red pepper flakes

1 small yellow onion, finely chopped

1 can (28 ounces) fire-roasted diced tomatoes, such as Muir Glen brand

20 fresh basil leaves (1 cup), shredded or torn

½ cup Parmigiano-Reggiano

½ pound smoked mozzarella, thinly sliced

6 cups mixed greens, any variety

2 tablespoons red wine vinegar

Heat an outdoor grill or indoor grill pan to high. Season the chicken with salt and pepper and drizzle with EVOO to keep it from sticking to the grill. Cook for 3 to 4 minutes on each side and transfer to a foil-covered platter to hold. If you are using a grill pan, cook the chicken in 2 batches if necessary. While the chicken cooks, make the sauce.

Place a medium pot on the stove over medium heat. Add 2 tablespoons of the EVOO (twice around the pan). Add the garlic, red pepper flakes, and onion. Cook for 10 minutes, stirring often. Add the tomatoes and heat through, 2 minutes. Wilt in the basil and season the sauce with salt and pepper.

Preheat the broiler to high.

Layer the chicken with the tomato sauce in a casserole dish. Top the casserole with Parmigiano and mozzarella. Brown the chicken parm casserole under the broiler for 3 minutes. Meanwhile, prepare the salad.

Place the greens in a salad bowl. Dress with the vinegar and the remaining 3 tablespoons of EVOO. Season with salt and pepper to taste.

Serve the chicken parm alongside a little salad.

CHAPTER 7

PASTA: COME HOME AGAIN!

Skip this section if you like,
but hey, this is an entire section of pasta dinners that use ONLY ½ POUND OF PASTA, ⅓ CUP COUSCOUS, or 1 CUP POLENTA for every 4 ENTRÉE PORTIONS. (Opportunities like these recipes do not come around often!) And if you're among those eating the "low-carb" replacement pastas, I contend that they taste more like paper than pasta and it's much smarter to eat a little of the real deal than to either go without or eat a lot of a bad fake!

Indian Spiced Vegetable and Couscous Pot

4 SERVINGS

3 tablespoons extra-virgin olive oil (EVOO) (3 times around the pan)
1-inch piece fresh gingerroot, peeled and minced or grated
1 teaspoon cumin seeds ($\frac{1}{3}$ palmful)
1 teaspoon crushed hot red pepper flakes
3 garlic cloves, crushed
1 head cauliflower, cut into florets
3 baby eggplants (1$\frac{1}{2}$ pounds), cut lengthwise into 1-inch wedges
1 small yellow onion, sliced
1 can (15 ounces) chickpeas
1 tablespoon ground coriander (a palmful)
1$\frac{1}{2}$ teaspoons turmeric (half a palmful)
1 teaspoon allspice ($\frac{1}{3}$ palmful)
1 teaspoon salt
1 cup chicken stock or broth
$\frac{1}{3}$ cup couscous
1 cup fresh basil leaves, torn or shredded, or $\frac{1}{4}$ cup chopped fresh cilantro, for garnish

Heat a deep nonstick skillet or pot (choose one that has a tight-fitting lid) over medium-high heat with the EVOO. When the EVOO ripples, stir in the ginger, cumin, red pepper flakes, and garlic, then add the cauliflower. Stir and sear the cauliflower, caramelizing it at the edges, 2 or 3 minutes, then push it to the side of the pan. Add the eggplant and onion and let them sit for

continued ....➤

3 minutes or so; they will caramelize a bit as well at their edges. Toss to combine the vegetables and add the chickpeas. In a small dish mix the coriander, turmeric, allspice, and salt. Stir in the spices and chicken stock and combine well. Bring the stock up to a bubble, 1 minute. Stir in the couscous and place a lid on the pan. Turn the heat off and let the pot stand for 5 minutes, covered. Remove the lid and fluff the mixture with a fork. Top each portion liberally with either torn or shredded basil or chopped cilantro.

Mediterranean Chicken and Sausage Couscous Pot

4 SERVINGS

- 2 tablespoons extra-virgin olive oil (EVOO) (twice around the pan)
- 4 hot Italian sausage links
- 4 6-ounce boneless, skinless chicken breasts, cut into ½-inch-thick slices
  Salt and freshly ground black pepper
- 2 teaspoons poultry seasoning (⅔ palmful)
- 1 medium yellow onion, thinly sliced
- 4 garlic cloves, finely chopped
- 2 celery ribs, chopped
- 1 small red bell pepper, cored, seeded, diced
- 1 10-ounce box frozen French-cut green beans, defrosted
- 1 cup chicken stock or broth
- ½ cup pitted kalamata olives
- 1 tablespoon capers, drained
- 2 oranges, zest reserved, peel and pith removed, cut into disks
- ⅓ cup plain couscous
- 2 handfuls fresh flat-leaf parsley leaves, coarsely chopped

Heat a large soup pot with the EVOO over medium-high heat. Add the sausage and brown all over for about 5 minutes. Move the sausage to one side of the pot and then add the sliced chicken. Season liberally with salt and pepper and add the poultry seasoning. Brown the chicken for about 3 minutes, then turn to brown opposite side. Add the onion, garlic, celery, and bell pepper. Cook for 2 minutes, stirring frequently. Add the defrosted green beans and the chicken stock. Bring the liquid up to a simmer, then add the olives, capers, orange slices, and orange zest, and stir to distribute. Stir in the couscous and cover the pot with a tight-fitting lid. Turn the stove off and let the pot sit covered for 5 minutes. Remove the lid and add the parsley while fluffing the dish with a serving fork. Serve immediately, making sure everyone gets a sausage link.

OPTIONS

If you've met your pork quota for the day or just don't do pork any day, try a flavored chicken or turkey sausage instead of the Italian sausage. Or, if you are suffering from chicken overload, then omit the chicken and the Italian sausage and go for a good-quality seafood sausage. Bump up the total amount of sausage, figuring about 3 seafood sausages per person.

TIDBIT

Broths and stocks have come a long way in the last few years, not only with their taste and consistency but with their packaging, too. They now come in resealable paper containers found on the soup aisle right alongside the cans. The paper containers make storage of remaining product easy; always keep some on hand in your refrigerator. Stocks especially add long-cooked flavor to any quick-cooking dish!

Eggplant and Wild Mushroom Pasta with Ricotta Salata

Leaving a little skin on the eggplants will add color and texture to the dish. The small, firm eggplants are not too bitter and when they are firm, they will not soak up as much oil, so they do not need to be salted and pressed. However, if you leave all the skin on, especially when you use baby egg-plant, the skin overpowers the flavor of the flesh and the texture is too tough, overall.

4 SERVINGS

2 ounces dried porcini mushrooms
1 cup chicken stock or broth
   Salt
2 medium vine-ripe tomatoes (½ pound)
½ pound cavatappi (corkscrew-shaped hollow pasta), or other shaped pasta
2 pounds (4 or 5) baby eggplants
3 tablespoons extra-virgin olive oil (EVOO) (three times around the pan)
3 garlic cloves, chopped
   Freshly ground black pepper
⅓ pound ricotta salata cheese, chopped and crumbled into small pieces (in specialty cheese case of market, among Italian selections)
1 cup (20 leaves) fresh basil, torn or shredded

Combine the porcinis and chicken stock in a small pot and bring up to a boil. Reduce the heat to lowest setting and let the mush-rooms soften and steep for 10 to 15 minutes, until very tender.

Place a pot of water on the stove to boil for the pasta. When it boils, salt the water to season it. Cut a small x into the bottom of the tomatoes and plunge them into the boiling pasta water for 30 seconds, then remove to a cutting board to cool. Add the cavatappi to the water and cook to al dente, or with a bite to it.

While the porcinis and pasta cook, trim half of the skin from the eggplant.

Heat a large nonstick skillet over medium-high heat. Cut the eggplant into 1- by $\frac{1}{2}$-inch bite-size pieces. Add the EVOO to the pan, followed by the garlic and eggplant. Turn and toss the eggplant and season it with salt and pepper. Let it brown lightly at edges, about 5 minutes, then reduce heat to medium low and continue to cook.

Pull the skins off the cooled tomatoes and cut them in half. Seed the tomatoes by gently squeezing them over the sink or a garbage bowl. Dice the tomatoes and add them to the cooking eggplant. Adjust seasoning with salt and pepper.

Remove the tender porcinis from the cooking broth and coarsely chop them. Add the broth and chopped mushrooms to the eggplant and tomatoes. Drain the pasta well and add the hot pasta to the pan. Toss to combine and coat and give the pasta a minute to soak in some juice. Add the ricotta salata and the basil; turn to wilt the basil, check the seasoning one last time, and serve.

OPTIONS

If your market has no ricotta salata (ricotta cheese that's been dried out a little), then use the same amount of feta but go easy on the salt you use in your preparation until your final adjustment because feta is saltier than ricotta salata. Tangy young goat cheese is an option, too. If you use goat cheese, toss and serve the dish without adding the goat cheese directly to the pan. Instead, garnish the individual plates with some crumbles, 2 ounces per portion. Goat cheese is too delicate to mix in as you would the feta or ricotta salata.

Spaghetti with Pancetta, Escarole, and Garlic Chips

4 SERVINGS

Salt
- ½ pound spaghetti, fresh or dried, your choice
- 3 tablespoons extra-virgin olive oil (EVOO)
- ¼ pound thickly sliced pancetta, chopped
- 6 to 8 garlic cloves, thinly sliced
- 1 teaspoon crushed hot red pepper flakes
- 2 large heads escarole, washed and drained, coarsely chopped
- ¾ cup chicken stock or broth (eyeball it)
- Zest and juice of 1 lemon
- Freshly ground black pepper
- 3 tablespoons butter
- ⅓ cup grated Parmigiano-Reggiano (a couple handfuls), plus some to pass

Fill a large pot with water, bring to a boil, and salt the water. Add the pasta and cook to al dente, with a bite to it.

While the pasta is working, heat a large skillet over medium heat with the EVOO (three times around the pan). Add the pancetta and cook until crisp, 2 to 3 minutes. Remove the pancetta from the skillet with a slotted spoon to a plate lined with a paper towel and reserve. Turn the heat on the pan back to low, then add the sliced garlic and cook until golden brown, 4 to 5 minutes. Remove the garlic chips from the pan to drain alongside the crispy pancetta. Turn the heat up to medium again, add the red pepper flakes, and cook for 30 seconds. Add the escarole, tossing it into the flavored oil to wilt in stages. Once all the escarole has fit into the pan, add the chicken stock, lemon juice, salt and pepper and cook for 2 minutes.

Drain the hot pasta well and add it to the escarole. Add the lemon zest and toss to distribute. Turn the heat off and add the butter and Parmigiano cheese, toss to melt. Toss in the crispy pancetta and garlic chips. Serve the spaghetti with more cheese to pass at the table.

Seared Tricolor Greens with Farfalle

4 SERVINGS

        Salt
½ pound farfalle (bow-tie) pasta
3 tablespoons extra-virgin olive oil (EVOO) (3 times around the pan)
4 thin slices prosciutto di Parma
3 garlic cloves, chopped
3 heads Belgian endive, chopped
2 heads radicchio, shredded
3 cups arugula leaves, chopped
        Freshly ground black pepper
1 cup chicken stock or broth
        Zest of 1 lemon
¼ cup chopped fresh flat-leaf parsley (a handful)
⅓ cup Parmigiano-Reggiano (a couple handfuls)

Heat a large pot of salted water to a boil, then add the pasta. Cook to al dente, or with a bite to it.

While the pasta cooks, prepare the greens: Heat a deep skillet over medium heat with the EVOO. Add the prosciutto in a single layer and fry until crisp and deep pink in color, a few minutes. Remove the prosciutto to a plate and let cool. Add the garlic next and sauté a minute or two. Raise the heat to medium high and add the endive. Toss and turn with tongs a minute or two, then add the radicchio and sear and toss for another two minutes. Add the arugula and toss again another minute. Season the tricolor greens (white, red, and green) with salt and pepper. Add the chicken stock to the pan and bring up to a boil.

Drain the pasta well and add it to the greens and broth. Add the lemon zest, parsley, and cheese and toss together 2 minutes. Transfer the pasta to a platter or individual plates. Break up the crisp prosciutto, snapping it into small pieces, and scatter it over the pasta for garnish.

Broccoli Rabe and Orecchiette

4 SERVINGS

Salt

½ pound orecchiette (little ear-shaped pastas), cooked al dente

2¼ to 2½ pounds (2 large bunches) broccoli rabe, ends trimmed, coarsely chopped

⅓ cup extra-virgin olive oil (EVOO) (4 or 5 times around the pan)

6 to 8 garlic cloves, finely chopped

1 teaspoon crushed hot red pepper flakes

½ cup freshly grated Parmigiano-Reggiano

Freshly ground black pepper

Place a pot of water on the stove to bring to a boil for the pasta. Cover the pot to bring water to a boil. Salt the water to season it and add the orecchiette. Cook al dente, with a bite to it. Heads up: Before draining the pasta, save a ladleful of the cooking water to add to the broccoli rabe.

Add the broccoli rabe and 2 to 3 cups water to a deep skillet. Cover the pan and bring the broccoli rabe to a boil. When the rabe wilts down into the pan, salt it. Simmer the rabe for about 7 minutes, until tender and no longer bitter. The color should remain deep green. Drain the rabe and reserve.

Return the deep skillet to the stove and place it over medium heat. Add the EVOO, garlic, and red pepper flakes and sauté for 2 to 3 minutes, stirring frequently. Add the broccoli rabe and turn to coat it in garlic oil. Add the ladleful of pasta water to the skillet; it will form a sauce as it emulsifies with the EVOO. Add the pasta, grated cheese, salt, and pepper, to taste and toss. Serve immediately.

TIDBIT

Add up to 1 pound of Italian hot or sweet bulk sausage, browned and crumbled, to make this dish stick to your ribs even more.

MOP-It-Up Pasta with Mushrooms, Onions, and Peppers

This dish combines fresh and pickled veggies. It tastes awesome hot or cold.

4 SERVINGS

Salt
½ pound cavatappi (hollow corkscrew pasta), or other shaped pasta
2 tablespoons extra-virgin olive oil (EVOO) (twice around the pan)
1 pound crimini (baby portobello) mushrooms, sliced
4 garlic cloves, chopped
1 large yellow onion, quartered and thinly sliced
1 red bell pepper, cored, seeded, quartered, and thinly sliced
1 cubanelle (long, light green mild Italian pepper), seeded and thinly sliced
Freshly ground black pepper
¼ cup jarred hot banana or hot cherry pepper rings, drained and chopped, plus a splash of their brine
1 cup jarred marinated mushrooms, drained and chopped
½ cup fresh flat-leaf parsley, coarsely chopped
⅓ cup grated Parmigiano-Reggiano (a couple handfuls)

Heat a pot of water to a boil for pasta. Season the water with some salt and add pasta. Cook the pasta al dente, or with a bite to it.

Preheat a large, deep skillet over medium-high heat. Add the EVOO and crimini mushrooms. Sauté until they start to become tender, 3 to 4 minutes, then add the garlic, stir for 30 seconds, and add the onion and fresh peppers. Season the MOP (mushrooms, onions, and peppers) with salt and pepper and cook 5 minutes more. Add the chopped hot peppers and a splash of their juice from the jar. Add the marinated mushrooms next and toss to combine.

Drain pasta and add to the MOP. Toss the whole thing together with the parsley and cheese and serve immediately.

Pesce Spada Pasta

4 SERVINGS

> Coarse salt
> 1/2 pound medium shell pasta
> 2 1/2 pounds swordfish steak, trimmed of skin and dark connective tissue
> 1/4 cup extra-virgin olive oil (EVOO)
> 4 to 6 garlic cloves, chopped
> 1 medium zucchini, diced
> 1/2 pint grape tomatoes
> 6 scallions, chopped
> 1 cup fresh basil (20 leaves), torn, or 1/4 cup fresh mint leaves (a handful), chopped
> 1/2 cup chopped fresh flat-leaf parsley (a handful)
> 1/2 cup dry white wine
> Freshly ground black pepper

Bring a large pot of water to a boil. Add a couple of teaspoons coarse salt to the boiling water, then add the pasta and cook for 8 or 9 minutes, al dente.

Cube the swordfish into bite-size pieces.

Heat a large, deep skillet over medium-high heat. Add the EVOO in a slow stream, then add the swordfish. Cook the fish until lightly browned on all sides. Remove with a slotted spoon to a plate and cover loosely with foil to hold.

Add the garlic, zucchini, and tomatoes to the pan and season with salt. Keep them moving and cook for 3 minutes. Add the scallions. Cook the vegetables for 2 minutes more, or until the skins of the tomatoes pop. Return the swordfish to the pan with the herbs. Douse the pan with the wine and lift the pan drippings. Add the hot drained starchy pasta and toss. Season with pepper and adjust salt to taste, then transfer to a huge bowl or platter and serve.

Tricolor Salad with Orange and Fennel
Insalata Tre Colore con Arancia e Finocchio

We eat a lot of swordfish when we are in Sicily, where my mom is from. She always orders a salad of oranges and fennel or oranges and onions to accompany it. When I cook swordfish anything at home, I always have oranges in the salad, for Mama.

4 SERVINGS

- 2 romaine lettuce hearts, chopped
- 2 cups arugula, torn
- 1 head radicchio, shredded
- 1/2 red onion, sliced
- 2 medium seedless oranges, ends trimmed, peel and pith cut away, sliced
- 1 large bulb fennel, core removed and thinly sliced
- 2 tablespoons red wine vinegar (eyeball it)
- 1/4 to 1/3 cup extra-virgin olive oil (EVOO) (3 or 4 times around the salad bowl)
  Salt and freshly ground black pepper

Combine the salad ingredients in a large bowl. Dress with the vinegar, then EVOO, tossing with your hands to evenly coat the salad, then season the salad with salt and pepper to taste. Serve.

Harvest Salad

4 SERVINGS

 2 tablespoons golden raisins, chopped
 1 small shallot, chopped
   Juice of $1/2$ lemon
 2 tablespoons red wine vinegar
 2 ounces chopped walnuts (on baking aisle)
 1 small crisp apple, quartered, cored, and thinly sliced
 1 Forelle or Seckel pear (the little guys), quartered, cored, and sliced
 3 cups arugula, chopped
 3 cups baby spinach, chopped
 $1/4$ cup extra-virgin olive oil (EVOO) (eyeball it)
   Salt and freshly ground black pepper

In a small bowl combine the raisins, shallot, lemon juice, and red wine vinegar and let stand for 10 minutes.

In a small skillet over medium-low heat toast the nuts for 3 to 4 minutes. Remove from the heat and reserve.

Combine the fruit with the greens. Whisk the EVOO into the dressing. Dress the salad and toss. Season with salt and pepper and garnish with the toasted walnuts.

Cauliflower-Pumpkin Pasta

Here again you can add in up to 1 pound Italian bulk sweet sausage, cooked and crumbled, and this becomes a hungry-man (or -woman) supersize meal!

4 SERVINGS

- 2 tablespoons extra-virgin olive oil (EVOO) (twice around the pan)
- 3 to 4 garlic cloves, chopped
- 1 large head cauliflower, cut into florets
- 1 cup chicken stock or broth
  Salt
- ½ pound cavatappi (hollow corkscrew pasta) or other shaped pasta
- 1 cup pumpkin purée (found on baking aisle; careful not to get pie filling)
- ¼ cup cream or half-and-half (eyeball it; a generous turn of the pan)
- ½ cup grated Parmigiano-Reggiano (3 handfuls, plus more to pass)
  A generous grating of fresh nutmeg
  Freshly ground black pepper
- 3 tablespoons chopped fresh sage leaves (4 or 5 sprigs)

Preheat a large skillet (choose one with a tight-fitting lid) over medium heat. Add the EVOO and garlic and cook for 1 minute. Add the cauliflower and turn to coat in EVOO. Add the chicken stock and bring up to a boil. Place the lid on the pan and simmer the cauliflower for 15 minutes, or until very tender.

Place a pot of water on to boil for the pasta. Put a lid on it and it will come up faster. Add some salt to season the water and add the pasta, cooking al dente, with a bite to it.

When the pasta is cooked and the cauliflower florets are very tender, remove the lid from the cauliflower and stir in the pumpkin purée and cream. Heat through, then drain off the pasta and add it to the cauliflower and pumpkin. Add the cheese, nutmeg, pepper, and sage. Toss, then season with salt to taste. Serve with extra cheese to pass at table with the Harvest Salad alongside.

Chicken Cacciatore and Rigatoni

4 BIG SERVINGS

Salt
½ pound rigatoni
2 tablespoons extra-virgin olive oil (EVOO) (twice around the pan)
1 pound chicken tenders, cut into 2-inch pieces
1 pound boneless, skinless chicken thighs, cut into 2-inch chunks
Freshly ground black pepper
¼ pound thick-cut pancetta, chopped
5 to 6 garlic cloves, chopped
1 teaspoon crushed hot red pepper flakes
4 portobello mushroom caps, halved, then thinly sliced across
½ cup dry red wine
1 cup beef stock
1 can (28 ounces) crushed tomatoes
A couple of handfuls fresh flat-leaf parsley, finely chopped
Grated Parmigiano-Reggiano to pass at table

Heat a pot of water to a boil for the pasta. When the water boils, season with salt and add the pasta. Cook to al dente, with a bite to it.

Meanwhile, heat a deep skillet over medium-high heat. Add the EVOO and chicken, white and dark meat, and season it with salt and pepper. Let the chicken sit for 3 to 4 minutes, then turn it and brown the opposite side for 2 to 3 minutes, seasoning it after the flip as well. Transfer the browned chicken to a plate and reserve. Add the pancetta to the pan and crisp it up, 2 or 3 minutes. Add the garlic and red pepper flakes, stir for 30 seconds, then add the mushrooms and brown for 8 to 10 minutes, stirring frequently, until deep brown and tender. Work on the Spinach with Lemon-Caper Butter, page 224, during your pocket of time here.

Season the mushrooms with salt and pepper after they've darkened. Deglaze the pan with the red wine and reduce it for 30 seconds, then stir in the stock and tomatoes. Bring the sauce up to a bubble and add the chicken back to the pan. Simmer the chicken for 5 minutes in the sauce to finish cooking through. Add the cooked pasta and parsley. Stir to combine and check seasoning. Serve with grated Parmigiano-Reggiano cheese and spinach.

OPTIONS

Hunter's chicken or cacciatore has always been made in my family with cut-up whole chickens, tomatoes, and lots of wild mushrooms (which my Sicilian grandfather knew how to forage for himself, deep in the woods where the hunters hang out). I never had peppers and onions in a cacciatore until I started eating out at Italian-American restaurants. Over the years I've met people who make it like I do and others who include only peppers and onions. If you like peppers and onions in your chicken cacciatore, hey, I'll never know, throw them in, too.

TIDBIT

Beef stock is used to make the dish taste as if it had been simmering a long time. I use beef rather than chicken stock to deepen the reddish brown tone of the sauce and to highlight the earthy, beef-like flavor of the mushrooms.

Spinach with Lemon-Caper Butter

4 SERVINGS

- 3 tablespoons butter, cut into small pieces
- Zest and juice of 1 lemon
- 3 tablespoons capers, drained and chopped
- 2 tablespoons chopped fresh thyme leaves, stripped from 4 to 5 sprigs
- 2 1-pound sacks triple-washed spinach
- Salt and freshly ground black pepper

Heat a large skillet over low heat. Melt the butter and add the lemon zest, capers, and thyme and let it hang out for 10 minutes, stirring occasionally.

Pick the tough larger stems from the spinach leaves and coarsely chop up the spinach. When you are ready to eat, raise the heat to medium and add the lemon juice to the pan. Add piles of spinach, turning it with tongs in the lemon-caper butter to wilt it in, then add more. When all of the spinach is in the pan, season it with salt and pepper and turn off the heat. Serve immediately.

Bucatini with Sausage, Peppers, and Onions

Bucatini looks like fat spaghetti that's hollow in the middle, like drinking straws made of pasta.

4 BIG SERVINGS

Salt
½ pound bucatini pasta
1 tablespoon extra-virgin olive oil (EVOO) (once around the pan)
1 pound bulk sweet Italian sausage
1 pound bulk hot Italian sausage
4 garlic cloves, chopped
1 large yellow onion, quartered, then thinly sliced
1 red bell pepper, cored, seeded, quartered, and thinly sliced
2 cubanelle peppers (long, light green mild Italian peppers), seeded and thinly sliced
1 can chunky-style crushed tomatoes
Freshly ground black pepper
⅓ cup grated Parmigiano-Reggiano (2 handfuls)
¼ cup fresh flat-leaf parsley (a couple handfuls), chopped
1 cup (20 leaves) fresh basil, torn or shredded

Bring a pot of water to a boil for the pasta and season the water with some salt. Cook bucatini al dente, with a bite to it.

continued ....➔

Heat a very large, deep skillet over medium-high heat. Add the EVOO and all of the sausage. Brown and crumble the sausage, 7 to 8 minutes. Remove from the pan to a plate lined with a paper towel and reserve. Drain off any pan drippings in excess of about 3 tablespoons. Add the garlic, onion, and peppers to the pan and toss and turn them in the fat, cooking them until just tender, 6 to 7 minutes. Combine the greens and herbs for the salad (see below) with your pocket of time here. You'll have time to spare. Got vino?

Once the peppers and onions are tender, add the tomatoes and heat them through. Add the sausage back and combine. Season the mixture with a little salt and lots of black pepper. Drain the pasta and add to pan. Stir in the cheese, parsley, and basil. Serve immediately.

Mixed Greens with Mixed Herbs Salad

4 SERVINGS

- 1 sack (6 cups) mixed greens, any variety or brand
- 1/2 cup (10 leaves) fresh basil, torn or shredded
- 1/2 cup fresh flat-leaf parsley (a few handfuls), coarsely chopped
- 10 fresh chive blades, snipped or chopped
- 4 to 5 sprigs fresh thyme, leaves stripped and chopped
- 2 tablespoons red wine vinegar, or juice of 1 lemon
  Extra-virgin olive oil (EVOO), to coat
  Salt and freshly ground black pepper

Combine the greens and herbs in a salad bowl.

When you are ready to eat, dress the greens with the vinegar or lemon juice first, then with EVOO, just enough to coat the greens but not enough to weigh them down. Season with salt and pepper to taste.

Roasted Baby Vegetables with Rosemary

Creamy Polenta and Bolognese Sauce

Roasted Baby Vegetables with Rosemary

4 SERVINGS

2½ pounds total weight of mixed baby vegetables, your choice: tiny zucchini, halved lengthwise; pattypan squash, halved across; baby eggplant, cut into 1-inch wedges lengthwise; whole baby carrots with tops, trimmed, peeled, and halved lengthwise; cippolini baby onions

5 to 6 garlic cloves, smashed

¼ cup extra-virgin olive oil (EVOO) (eyeball it)

3 tablespoons finely chopped fresh rosemary (a handful of leaves)
Salt and freshly ground black pepper

Preheat the oven to 500°F.

Combine the veggies on a large baking sheet and toss with the garlic, EVOO, rosemary, salt, and pepper. Roast for 15 minutes. Remove from the oven. Let stand for 5 minutes, then serve.

Creamy Polenta and Bolognese Sauce

Allspice is the secret ingredient here. In Italian cooking, it is VITAL to have a secret ingredient in your meat sauce.

4 SERVINGS

- 4 cups chicken stock or broth
- 1/4 cup heavy cream
- 5 garlic cloves, crushed
- Coarse salt and freshly ground black pepper
- 1 tablespoon extra-virgin olive oil (EVOO) (once around the pan)
- 1/2 to 1 teaspoon crushed hot red pepper flakes
- 1 pound ground sirloin (90% lean ground beef)
- 1/2 pound ground pork
- 1/2 pound ground veal
- 1 small yellow onion, chopped
- 1/2 cup shredded carrots (on salad bar in produce aisle), chopped
- 1 celery rib, finely chopped
- 1 tablespoon fresh thyme leaves, chopped
- 1/2 teaspoon allspice (a couple healthy pinches)
- 1/2 cup dry red wine
- 1 can (28 ounces) crushed tomatoes
- A handful of chopped fresh flat-leaf parsley
- 1 cup quick-cooking polenta (in Italian foods or specialty foods aisles)
- 1/2 cup grated Parmigiano-Reggiano or Romano cheese, plus some to garnish

For the creamy polenta, combine 3 cups of the chicken stock, the cream, 1 of the crushed garlic cloves, salt, and pepper in a sauce-pot over medium-low heat. Bring up to a gentle simmer and lower the heat so it is barely bubbling, then start the Bolognese sauce.

Heat a deep skillet or heavy-bottomed pot over medium-high heat. Go once around the pan with a slow stream of EVOO. Add the remaining crushed garlic and the red pepper flakes and infuse the oil for 15 seconds. Add the beef, pork, and veal and break the meat up with a wooden spoon. Brown the meats for 3 minutes, then add the onion, carrots, celery, thyme, allspice, salt, and pepper and continue browning for 5 minutes more. Use the pocket of time to make the roasted veggies, page 227.

When the vegetables are tender, add the wine and scrape up the drippings, then add the remaining 1 cup of chicken stock and reduce for 5 minutes. Add the tomatoes and reduce heat to low. Simmer for 5 to 10 minutes to combine flavors. Finish the sauce with the chopped parsley.

As the Bolognese sauce is in its last 5 to 10 minutes of cooking time, whisk the polenta into the simmering seasoned chicken stock–cream mixture in a steady stream and stir constantly until the polenta can thickly coat the back of a spoon. Taste for seasoning and adjust with salt and pepper. If you find the polenta is thickening up so much that it is not creamy and it is becoming stiff, you can loosen it with a little more chicken stock or water. Turn the heat off and stir in the cheese.

To serve, divide the creamy polenta among 4 bowls, top the polenta with a BIG serving of the Bolognese sauce, and garnish with some more grated cheese.

TIDBIT

Polenta's like a magical porridge when you are in a carbohydrate-depravation depression. It is delicious and easy, and when you cook it creamy-style, a little dry polenta goes a long way in the tasty cooking liquid. I eat it guilt free!

Saabs and Meatballs: Things-to-Thank-the-Swedes-for Menu

Red Radish, Red Apple, and Red Onion Salad

Swedish Meatballs on Noodles

Red Radish, Red Apple, and Red Onion Salad

4 SERVINGS

- 6 radishes, thinly sliced
- 1 red-skinned apple, your favorite variety, quartered, cored, and thinly sliced
- 2 teaspoons fresh lemon juice or a wedge of fresh lemon
- ½ red onion, thinly sliced
- 1 head red romaine lettuce or red leaf lettuce, chopped

DILL AND POPPY SEED DRESSING

- 3 tablespoons red wine vinegar
- 2 teaspoons honey (a drizzle)
- 1 teaspoon salt
- ¼ cup extra-virgin olive oil (EVOO)
- ½ cup sour cream
- 1 teaspoon poppy seeds
- 2 tablespoons chopped fresh dill or 2 teaspoons dried

In a large bowl combine the radishes, apple (coated in the lemon juice to retard browning), and onion with the chopped lettuce. In a small bowl, combine the vinegar with the honey and salt. Whisk in the EVOO. Stir in the sour cream, poppy seeds, and dill. Pour the dressing evenly over the salad, toss, and serve.

Swedish Meatballs on Noodles

1¾ pounds ground sirloin

1 large egg, beaten

¼ cup plain bread crumbs

½ small yellow onion, chopped

A healthy grating of nutmeg

½ cup fresh flat-leaf parsley leaves (3 handfuls), chopped

Freshly ground black pepper

2 tablespoons extra-virgin olive oil (EVOO)

2 cups beef stock

1 tablespoon red currant or grape jelly

1 cup heavy cream or sour cream

½ pound wide egg noodles

Salt

2 tablespoons butter

8 cornichons or 6 baby gherkins, chopped, for garnish

Place the ground sirloin in a large mixing bowl and punch a well into the center. Fill the well with the egg, bread crumbs, onion, nutmeg, half of the chopped parsley, and a little salt and pepper. Mix up the meatball ingredients until well combined, yet not overmixed. Divide the mix into 4 equal parts. Roll each part into 6 balls. Heat a large nonstick skillet over medium-high heat with the EVOO. Add the meatballs and brown on all sides, about 5 minutes, giving the pan a good shake now and then. Add the stock, jelly, and heavy cream or sour cream. Bring it up to a bubble, then reduce heat to a simmer and cook for 8 to 10 minutes.

Place a large pot of water on to boil. Add the noodles and season the water with salt. Cook until just tender, 5 to 6 minutes. Drain the egg noodles and shake dry. Put the noodles back in the hot pot and add the remaining chopped parsley and the butter and season with salt and pepper. Stir until the butter has melted. Top the noodles with the meatballs, their sauce, and pickles.

PASTA: COME HOME AGAIN!

Great Goulash and Caper-Capped Salad

Bibb Lettuce Salad with Caper Dressing Caps

Ground Turkey Paprikash-Goulash with Macaroni

Bibb Lettuce Salad with Caper Dressing Caps

4 SERVINGS

- 2 small heads Bibb lettuce, cores removed, halved
- 4 radishes, sliced
- ¼ English (seedless) cucumber (the one wrapped in plastic), sliced
- 4 tablespoons capers, drained
- 2 tablespoons fresh dill or 2 teaspoons dried
- ¼ cup chopped fresh flat-leaf parsley (a handful)
- 1 small shallot, chopped
- 3 tablespoons red wine vinegar
   Salt and freshly ground black pepper
- ⅓ cup extra-virgin olive oil (EVOO) (eyeball it)

Place each half-head of lettuce on individual plates cut side down so the lettuce forms a mound on the plate. Arrange the radish and cucumber slices around each lettuce mound. Place the capers, dill, parsley, shallot, vinegar, salt, and pepper in a blender. Turn the blender on and stream in the EVOO. Test for seasonings in the dressing. Spoon the dressing evenly over the salads, capping the lettuce.

Ground Turkey Paprikash-Goulash with Macaroni

4 SERVINGS

- ½ pound rigate (ribbed elbow macaroni)
  - Salt
- 1 tablespoon extra-virgin olive oil (EVOO) (once around the pan)
- 1 tablespoon butter
- 2½ pounds ground lean white-meat turkey
- 4 garlic cloves, chopped
- 1 medium onion, chopped
- 1 red bell pepper, cored, seeded, and chopped
- 2 tablespoons sweet paprika (2 palmfuls)
- 2 teaspoons ground cumin (⅔ palmful)
- 2 teaspoons dried marjoram (⅔ palmful)
- 2 teaspoons freshly ground black pepper (⅔ palmful)
- 2 cups chicken stock or broth
- 1 cup sour cream
- 2 tablespoons finely chopped fresh dill
- 2 tablespoons finely chopped fresh flat-leaf parsley (a generous handful)

Bring a pot of water to a boil for the pasta. When it comes to a boil, add the pasta and salt to season the cooking water. Cook the pasta for 6 minutes, al dente.

While the water comes to a boil and the pasta cooks, heat a deep skillet over medium-high heat. Add the EVOO, then butter, then ground meat. Break up the meat and crumble, 2 to 3 minutes. Add the garlic, onion, bell pepper, and seasonings to the turkey. Cook for 5 or 6 minutes, then add the chicken stock and sour cream. Bring to a bubble and reduce heat to low. Add the cooked pasta and stir. Let the pasta absorb some sauce, a minute or so. Adjust the seasonings and serve. Garnish with chopped parsley.

CHAPTER 8

DESSERTS? YES, DESSERTS

No, really. Way-low carb,
way-good, and so easy, even a nonbaker
(like me) can make them!

Ginger-Poached Pears with Ricotta and Blueberries

This dish is so simple, yet it could be served at any elegant dinner party. It is equally good warm or cold and makes a great addition to a Sunday brunch.

4 SERVINGS

1 cup water
1-inch piece fresh gingerroot, peeled and sliced
2 tablespoons sugar
Zest of 1 lemon
2 firm pears, such as Bosc or Anjou, peeled, cored, and coarsely chopped
¾ cup whole-milk ricotta
Dash ground cinnamon
½ cup fresh blueberries

In a saucepan, bring the water, ginger, sugar, and lemon zest to a boil over medium-high heat. Add the pears, and when the pot returns to a boil, reduce the heat to medium-low to maintain the simmer. Cook the pears until very soft when pierced with a knife (but not falling apart), 12 to 15 minutes. Remove the pan from the heat and, using a slotted spoon, divide the pears among 4 dessert cups or ice cream dishes.

Add the ricotta and cinnamon to the warm syrup and stir gently until very smooth. Top the pears with the warm cheese mixture, then tumble some fresh blueberries over each serving.

Mascarpone Parfait with Citrus Salad

Sweet, tart, crunchy, and creamy, this dessert is just about perfect, and low-carb to boot! This is perfect for Sunday brunch, or as a light and refreshing ending to a heavy winter meal. Try it with blood oranges when they're in season, or your favorite combination of citrus fruits.

4 SERVINGS

- 8 vanilla or plain meringue cookies
- 8 ounces mascarpone cheese
- 2 tablespoons honey
- 1 large orange
- 1 ruby grapefruit
  Zest of 1 lime
- 1 tablespoon chopped fresh mint, plus sprigs for garnishing

Put the cookies into a food storage bag and crush them with a rolling pin or the back of a pan. Set aside. In a bowl, mix together the mascarpone and 1 tablespoon of the honey. Set this aside also as you make the citrus salad.

Slice the top and bottom off the orange and grapefruit so that the fruit sits upright. Remove the peel by slicing around the flesh, cutting deep enough to remove the outer membrane along with the peel. Cut the segments away from the membrane and transfer to a bowl. Squeeze a little of the juice from the remains of the orange and grapefruit over the segments. Stir in the lime zest, remaining tablespoon of honey, and mint.

To assemble the parfaits, divide the crushed meringue cookies among 4 tall, narrow glasses or ice cream dishes. Put ¼ cup of the mascarpone on top of the cookies in each glass, followed by one fourth of the citrus salad. Garnish with a mint sprig and serve immediately.

Very Berry Crumble

I like to use frozen berries for this crumble. Not only can I have it any time of year, but the juices left in the bag after thawing provide sweetness (without adding a lot of sugar) and sauce for the crumble.

4 SERVINGS

CRUMBLE TOPPING

¾ cup sliced almonds, lightly crushed

⅓ cup quick-cooking oats

2 teaspoons sugar

Hefty pinch of ground cinnamon

Pinch of fresh grated nutmeg

2 tablespoons butter, softened, plus more for greasing ramekins

FILLING

1 10-ounce bag frozen raspberries, thawed

1 10-ounce bag frozen blueberries, thawed

1 tablespoon sugar

1 tablespoon cornstarch

Preheat the oven to 375°F. Grease four 6-ounce ramekins and transfer them to a foil-lined baking sheet and set aside.

To make the topping, in a bowl combine the almonds, oats, sugar, and spices. Add the butter, and, with your fingers or a fork, rub the butter into the dry ingredients until large, coarse crumbs form. Set aside while you make the filling.

To make the filling, put the berries into a strainer set over a bowl to catch the juices. Add the sugar and cornstarch to the juices and whisk until smooth and the starch dissolves. Gently fold the berries back into their juices, and divide the mixture among the greased ramekins. Top each filled dish with one fourth of the crumble topping and place on the baking sheet. Bake until bubbling hot and the topping is golden, about 20 minutes. Allow the crumbles to cool for at least 10 minutes before serving.

Chocolate Banana "Eggrolls" with Cinnamon Cream

4 SERVINGS

EGGROLLS

4 sheets (14 x 9 inches) phyllo dough (available in the freezer section), thawed
Butter-flavored cooking spray
2 ounces bittersweet chocolate, chopped
1 banana, peeled
1 teaspoon brown sugar
Ground cinnamon

CINNAMON CREAM

⅓ cup heavy cream
1 teaspoon brown sugar
Ground cinnamon

Preheat the oven to 350°F. Line a baking sheet with parchment paper and set aside.

Lay a phyllo sheet lengthwise on a large work surface and spray it with cooking spray. Top the sheet with another phyllo layer and spray it again. Cut the sheet in half from top to bottom. Repeat the process with the 2 remaining phyllo sheets. (You will have 4 phyllo rectangles lying vertically on the work surface.) Sprinkle a quarter of the chopped chocolate along the bottom edge of each phyllo rectangle.

Halve the banana lengthwise and cut each half into two pieces. Lay a piece, cut side down, on top of the chocolate on the bottom edge of each phyllo rectangle. Sprinkle a little brown sugar over the banana. Fold about an inch of the side edges of the phyllo over the ends of the banana, and then roll the packet to form an eggroll shape. Repeat with the remaining bananas and transfer them to the baking sheet. Spray each roll with a little more cooking spray, then sprinkle a little cinnamon over each. Bake until golden brown and crisp, about 12 minutes. Remove from the oven and let cool for about 10 minutes before serving.

Meanwhile, in a mixing bowl, whisk the cream, brown sugar, and a couple dashes of cinnamon together until the brown sugar dissolves. Continue whisking until the cream thickens and begins to hold soft peaks. Transfer to a small bowl and sprinkle a little more cinnamon on the top.

To serve, cut the eggrolls in half diagonally and place on a platter with the cream "dipping sauce."

Spiced Plum Crepes with Port Syrup

4 SERVINGS

    4 red plums, pitted and thinly sliced
  ½ cup port wine
  ¼ cup water
    1 tablespoon brown sugar
       1-inch piece cinnamon stick
    3 whole cloves
    3 whole black peppercorns
    4 ready-made crepes (from the bakery section)
       Whipped cream, for garnish

Put the plums, port, water, brown sugar, cinnamon, cloves, and peppercorns in a saucepan and bring to a boil over medium-high heat. Reduce the heat to maintain a gentle simmer and cook until the plums are soft but still hold their shape, 12 to 15 minutes. Transfer the plums to a bowl with a slotted spoon, remove the spices, and

continued ....➤

cover to keep warm. Increase the heat to medium-high and cook the remaining liquid until thick and syrupy, 3 to 4 minutes.

To serve, put a crepe on each of 4 dessert plates. Put a spoonful of plums on one quarter of each crepe. Then, fold the crepe over the filling to create a triangle shape. (The crepes can also be served folded in half like an omelet, or rolled.) Top each filled crepe with a dollop of whipped cream, then drizzle the warm port syrup over the top of each.

Cocoa-Nutty Haystacks

These crunchy, chewy treats are sure to satisfy any sweet tooth! Try adding dried cherries or chopped bittersweet chocolate (depending on how many carbs you've had for dinner).

12 COOKIES

    1 whole egg
    1 egg white
    1 tablespoon sugar
   ½ teaspoon vanilla
    1 tablespoon cocoa powder
    1 cup sliced almonds, slightly crushed
   ¾ cup shredded sweetened coconut

Preheat the oven to 350°F. Line a baking sheet with parchment paper and set aside.

In a bowl, whisk together the egg, egg white, sugar, and vanilla until smooth and the sugar is dissolved. Add the cocoa powder and whisk vigorously until the batter is smooth. Stir in the almonds and coconut until well combined. Use a mini ice cream scoop or spoon to drop 12 tablespoon-size mounds onto the baking sheet. Bake until they begin to brown, 10 to 12 minutes. Let the cookies cool for 5 minutes on the pan before transferring to a rack to cool completely.

Nutty "Creamsicle" Pie

This recipe takes a little planning, as it needs to chill before cutting. It comes together in a snap, however, and is truly yummy—just like the Creamsicles you had as a kid!

8 SERVINGS

- 1¹⁄₂ cups (6 ounces) pecan halves
- 1 tablespoon sugar
- 6 tablespoons (³⁄₄ stick) butter, melted
- 8 ounces whipped cream cheese
- Zest and juice of 1 orange
- 1 packet (.03 ounces) sugar-free orange gelatin
- 1 cup heavy cream
- Fresh mint sprigs, for garnish (optional)

Preheat the oven to 350°F.

In the bowl of a mini food processor, chop the pecans until very fine and transfer to a 9-inch pie plate. Stir the sugar into the pecans and add the melted butter. Mix until the pecans are completely moistened. Press the nuts evenly into the pan with your fingers to create an even crust. Bake until the crust is golden, 6 to 8 minutes. Set aside to cool. (Pop it into the freezer or fridge to speed up this process.)

When the crust is completely cool, make the filling. Mix the cream cheese together with the orange juice in a bowl until smooth. Open the gelatin packet, add ¹⁄₂ teaspoon to the cream cheese mixture, and stir vigorously until well mixed. Pour the mixture into the chilled crust and spread it evenly with a spoon or spatula. Pour the heavy cream and remaining gelatin into a clean bowl. With an electric hand mixer, beat the cream until soft peaks form. Pour the cream over the cream cheese filling and spread it decoratively over the top. Sprinkle the orange zest over the pie and refrigerate for at least 2 hours.

To serve, cut into 8 slices, plate, and garnish with a sprig of mint.

Mini Chocolate Cherry Bites

A classic—like biting into a chocolate-covered cherry, only lower in carbs, and better!

8 MINI TARTS

- 4 ounces bittersweet chocolate, chopped
- 1 tablespoon whole milk
- 1/2 cup finely chopped pecans
- 1/2 cup sugar-free cherry jam
  Spray whipping cream (the real kind in the can in the dairy section)

Spray a mini muffin tin with nonstick cooking spray and set aside.

Put the chocolate and milk into a heat-safe bowl and place over a pot of gently simmering water. Stir until melted and smooth. This can also be done in the microwave in a glass or plastic bowl by heating the chocolate on Low for a minute or two, stirring it until melted and smooth. Next, stir in the pecans until well mixed. Put a heaping tablespoon of the mixture into 8 portions of the muffin tin. Using the handle of a wooden spoon, lightly press the mixture into the sides and bottom of each portion, creating a cup shape. Chill for 15 minutes.

Once chilled, use a thin butter knife or icing spatula to release the chocolate cups from the tin. Place them on a serving platter. Fill each cup with a tablespoon of the jam, and top with a spritz of whipped cream.

Creamy-Crunchy Peach Tarts

4 SERVINGS

- ¼ cup (2 ounces) sliced almonds
- 2 sheets (14 x 9 inches) phyllo dough (available in the freezer section), thawed
  Butter-flavored cooking spray
- 2 teaspoons sugar
- 1 ripe peach, pitted and finely chopped
- ½ cup whipped cream cheese
  Ground cinnamon or nutmeg

Preheat the oven to 350°F. Line a baking sheet with parchment paper and set aside.

Put the almonds into a bag and crush them with your hand. Lay one sheet of phyllo onto a work surface and spray it with cooking spray. Sprinkle about ½ teaspoon sugar over the phyllo, along with a small handful of crushed almonds. Lay the second phyllo sheet over the top, spray it, and top with another ½ teaspoon of sugar and more almonds, reserving the remaining almonds to garnish the dessert. Cut the phyllo into quarters. Transfer the pieces to the baking sheet. Using your fingers, "scrunch" each piece to give it a ruffled appearance. Bake the phyllo just until brown, about 5 minutes. (Watch carefully—these can burn easily!)

Meanwhile, put the peach pieces into a bowl and stir in the remaining teaspoon of sugar. Mash part of the peaches with a fork to get the juices flowing and let the fruit sit for a few minutes. Transfer about one third of the peaches to another bowl along with the cream cheese. Stir the mixture vigorously until the cheese is smooth.

To serve, put a crispy phyllo piece on each of 4 plates. Top each with one fourth of the cheese mixture, then one fourth of the sweetened peaches. Sprinkle with cinnamon or nutmeg.

Stuffed Roasted Strawberries

4 SERVINGS

- 12 extra-large strawberries (the bigger the better!)
- 1 to 2 ounces bittersweet chocolate, chopped
- 1 teaspoon sugar (optional)
  - Spray whipping cream (the real kind in the can in the dairy section)
  - Cocoa powder, for garnish

Preheat the oven to 400°F.

Slice the tops of the berries off just below the stem. Cut the tips off (about ¼ inch), so that the berries will sit upright. Next, use a small spoon or a melon-ball scoop to hollow out the strawberries, working from their tops, to create a cavity in each one. Stuff some chocolate into the cavity of each strawberry and place them upright in a baking dish. Lightly sprinkle the berries with sugar, if using. Roast the berries until soft and the chocolate is melted, 10 to 12 minutes.

To serve, place 3 strawberries on a dessert plate in a triangle. If the berries have given off liquid in the baking dish, spoon it over them. Spray a small mound of cream in the center of the berries, and top each berry with a rosette of cream. Sift a little cocoa powder over the plate, and serve!

RECIPISTORY

This is an inside-out version of chocolate-dipped strawberries. Roasting the fruit brings out even more flavor and juiciness. You'll never settle for plain old dipped berries again! You can use any type of chocolate (milk, white, or semisweet), but remember bittersweet chocolate has less sugar and is lower in carbs.

INDEX

245